DINING
FABULOUS TABLE SETTINGS FOR SPECIAL OCCASIONS
IN STYLE

DINING

FABULOUS TABLE SETTINGS FOR SPECIAL OCCASIONS

IN STYLE

by Jim Kemp

Sterling Publishing Co., Inc.   New York

A QUARTO BOOK

Copyright © 1986 by Quarto Marketing Ltd.

Published in the United States by
Sterling Publishing Co., Inc.
Two Park Avenue
New York, N.Y. 10016

Library of Congress Cataloging in Publication Data
Kemp, Jim.
  Dining in style.
  Includes index.
  1. Table setting and decoration.   I. Title.
   TX871.K45   1986   642'.7   86-5821
        ISBN 0-8069-6358-1

DINING IN STYLE: *Fabulous Table Settings for Special Occasions*
was prepared and produced by
Quarto Marketing Ltd.
15 West 26th Street
New York, N.Y. 10010

Editor: Louise Quayle
Copy Editor: Mary Forsell
Art Director/Designer: Mary Moriarty
Photo Researcher: Susan M. Duane
Production Manager: Karen L. Greenberg
Art Production: Christine M. Cancelli

Typeset by BPE Graphics, Inc.
Color separations by South Seas Graphic Art Company
Printed and bound in Hong Kong by Leefung-Asco Printers Ltd.

Dedication

For C. Richard King, Ph.D.

Acknowledgments

THE WORK OF PREPARING DINING IN STYLE WAS greatly aided by a number of people who shared their thoughts and expertise. For patiently sitting through a series of interviews, I am indebted to four stylists: Kim Freeman and Sheilah Shulman of New York City; Becky McDermott of Greenwich, Connecticut; and L.A. Clever of Houston, Texas. Interior designers Sam Botero in New York City and Gerrie Bremmerman of New Orleans graciously added their creative ideas as did Mark Leskowski of Lars and Penates caterers in New York City.

For background information, table-setting ideas, and entree into the world of tablewares, I also wish to thank Trish Foley, editor of *House Beautiful's Home Decorating* magazine and author of *Having Tea*, to be published by Clarkson N. Potter, Incorporated; Deborah Slotnik of *Home Furnishings Daily*; Nina Kaminer, president of Nike Communications in New York City; and Tessie Frugé of the Rives Frugé public relations agency in Houston.

Technical assistance was provided by representatives of the manufacturing and retailing communities including Richard Babick, research manager, Lenox Incorporated; Al Donnelly of the Corning Glass Works; Frank J. McIntosh of the shops of the same name; and Ronald A. Fippinger, managing director of the National Housewares Manufacturers Association. I also wish to thank Ed Gillies of Contempo and Don Kramer for Jeff MacNamara for providing photographs.

Dining in Style could not have been completed without the help and encouragement of the staff at Quarto Marketing Ltd., under whose auspices the book was written. I am especially appreciative to Marta Hallett, former associate publisher for assigning me the project; my editor, Louise Quayle; photo researcher Susan Duane; art director Mary Moriarty, former art director Richard Boddy and the copyeditor Mary Forsell.

Other unsung heroes of *Dining in Style* also deserve my thanks: interior designer Ferne Goldberg for saving the research files from an untimely death in her incinerator . . . co-workers Richard Horn and Susan Boyle for their unwavering support . . . and, finally, Pat Shannon and Mike Coleman, who, with only occasional grumbling, endured each trauma *du jour.*

C O N T E N T S

CONTENTS

Introduction

MORE AND MORE, THE DINING TABLE IS BECOMING the heart of the home. Busy two-career couples and families with independently minded children often find that meals are the *only* times when they can be together. Add to that the high cost of treating friends to dinner in a good restaurant, and it is easy to understand why home buyers in a recent survey cited entertaining as their favorite at-home activity. As a result hostesses—and hosts—are taking extra care in the preparation and presentation of food as well as the setting in which it is enjoyed.

Your preference for entertaining may range from a casual buffet before a football game to the classic favorite, the sit-down dinner. Regardless of the occasion, it presents the opportunity to show off your creativity and flair with a stylish table setting. "An evening with friends is more than a meal—it's a memory," notes L.A. Clever, a Houston photo stylist well known for her sophisticated table settings. Echoes another stylist, Kim Freeman of New York City: "When you sit down at a nicely set table with flowers and candles, you know that your hosts care about you and want you to feel welcome."

The best table settings are creative, stylish, and appropriate. A friend once complained that at a dinner party he attended, the host—perhaps in an attempt to show off—set the table with his best china, silver, and crystal. My friend was duly impressed until the meal was presented. "The guy did all that to serve lasagna!" he groaned.

Many newlyweds will recognize this situation. Though they may have wedding gifts of formal tableware, they lack the stainless-steel flatware, earthenware plates, and other items for the casual entertaining that is so popular today. Many interior designers suggest that rather than buy tableware to suit the occasion, make the meal a complement to the tableware you already have. The visual appeal of lasagna is enlivened when it is made with fresh green noodles and served to guests on a china platter garnished with fresh basil and sliced tomatoes. You want your dishes to offset the food and the food to offset the dishes. Sprigs of herbs arranged on the platter and flowers tucked in the napkins are simple touches that can make the dining experience spectacular.

Another approach is to garnish a dish of fruit with the blossom of an exotic flower in the tradition of the ancient Egyptians. Still applicable today, this and many other ideas can be borrowed directly from history. As a matter of fact, many earthenware casseroles imported from continental Europe resemble the ceramic storage pots made by the ancient Greeks. The Romans used fruit dishes in the shape of a shell—a motif that is readily found in the contemporary marketplace—made in silver, pottery, and glass. The basic shape of modern-day glassware was developed in the eighth century, while covering the table with a damask cloth dates from the twelfth century. The Renaissance gave us the fork and the napkin, and the latter was arranged in elaborate folds in the seventeenth century to complement dramatically swirled candelabra and ornate sugar bowls.

In the 1600s, the Dutch East India Company imported the famous blue-and-white

porcelains from the Orient to Holland, then England, and, in turn, to the British colonies in the New World. The greater availability of this chinaware spurred enthusiasm for more, and Europeans attempted to duplicate the formula. After many failures, the process was copied by John Boettger of Dresden, Germany, in 1709, which revolutionized the production of tableware. Factories were founded in Meissen, Germany, and, later, in England. Tea drinking became fashionable, spurring an entirely new line of tableware—teapots, bowls, and caddies.

The classical chinaware designs of the late 1700s extended into the early 1800s when Egyptian motifs in the form of sphinx-like bases for candelabras and centerpieces were added to the design repertoire. The invention of the machine in the 1800s sparked the manufacture of a proliferation of decorative motifs on china, including flowers, birds, rocks, and seashells. Much of this tableware is lovely; much is unabashed kitsch with overwrought designs and unrestrained decoration.

The Victorian Age was a riot of revivalism as historical styles from Greek to Renaissance to Oriental were reinterpreted en masse for home furnishings. The Oriental influence, in part, led to the development of the free-flowing lines and organic forms of the Art Nouveau style near the end of the century.

Tableware through most of the twentieth century has mirrored the prevailing style of interior decoration—Art Deco in the 1930s, the Modern movement as embodied in the work of the Bauhaus architects between the two World Wars, and the sculptural, free-form designs by mass manufacturers in the 1950s and 60s. Unlike past decades, with their clearly defined styles and trends, interior design in the 1980s is in a period of flux. The influence of Modernism is waning as the definitive style in architecture, yet no other style has so captured and dominated the imagination of professionals in the field or the general public. Today's preferences span many styles—country, contemporary, and, as always, the avant-garde. Underlying all of these influences is the powerful emotional pull exerted by traditionalism throughout all the fine and decorative arts.

Tableware is now available in a variety of materials from porcelain to plastic. Some china designs date back two hundred years; others are new this season. While Tiffany & Company sells the classic black basalt dishes designed by Josiah Wedgwood in the eighteenth century, it also offers the thoroughly contemporary work of Elsa Peretti. Other well-known designers are creating lines of dinnerware expressly for major manufacturers. Both Jack Lenor Larsen, an innovator in the home textiles industry, and men's fashion designer Daniel Hechter have worked with Mikasa on extensive programs encompassing coordinated dinnerware, stemware, and flatware. The New York City firm of Swid-Powell Design manufactures tablewares by noted architects including Richard Meier, Robert Venturi, Steven Holl, and Charles Gwathmey.

Craftspeople have added to the excitement with limited-edition and even one-of-a-kind ceramic pieces that can be custom-ordered for reasonable prices or bought in craft galleries and specialty stores.

Mass-produced patterns that are no longer manufactured are again in vogue. Russel Wright's famous dinnerware, American Modern, designed for Steubenville—once given away to patrons by movie theater managers—is eminently collectible and increasingly expensive. The humble Fiesta-ware made in the 1940s is showcased in the windows of nostalgia-oriented shops catering to collectors and antiques buffs. The popularity of these old pieces has inspired new versions that are sold in kitchen-specialty shops and department stores.

Long ago, eating utensils expanded far

beyond the term ''silverware'' to encompass a variety of materials. Besides classic sterling silver, silver plate, and stainless-steel flatware, manufacturers such as Towle Silversmiths offer stainless decorated with gold-plated handle accents. Ricci Silversmiths produces traditionally inspired patterns fabricated in gold as well as in silver. Makers of stainless-steel flatware have introduced elaborately detailed patterns that bring new elegance to the table. And many long-time silver manufacturers are updating their traditional lines with contemporary sterling designs that artfully blend a contemporary shape with detailing adapted from earlier designs.

Barware is easily the fastest growing segment of the glassware business as cleverly packaged sets of wine, beer, and liqueur glasses—many of them handblown—enter the market. Contemporary-styled crystal stemware for the table is manufactured in a number of countries, including the Eastern bloc, and exported to Britain and the United States where it is often sold at extremely reasonable prices. Other plastic and glass barware reflects the visually harsh designs made famous by the Italian collaborative called Memphis.

Manufacturers are also constantly searching for salable designs of the past. The Schott-Sweisel glassworks, makers of the modern classic Jena teapot, now offers crystal stemware recut from Art Deco molds, a perfect addition to a 1930s-style table setting.

The department store is the most popular retailer of tableware. With a wide variety of brands and an extensive inventory, it is a veritable one-stop shopping center for every sort of dinnerware from the finest china to the most casual pottery. However, don't limit your shopping to large stores only as inventive and beautiful tableware is carried by many specialty stores.

Kitchen-supply stores are wonderful sources of lovely and inexpensively priced china, crystal, and stainless-steel flatware. Craft galleries and boutiques are another exciting place to find exquisitely designed wares for the table. Be on the lookout, too, for tableware in stores known for other types of merchandise.

Blending all these disparate elements together into a table setting that reflects your individuality is an exciting challenge. In *Dining in Style* you will find an array of enticing table designs to help you define your own personal style. You will also encounter inventive ideas that you can adapt to your entertaining needs, budget, and life-style, whether you prefer to host elegant dinner parties at home or picnics on the beach.

Just as important as the table-setting ideas is the exhaustive directory of tableware sources. These include mail-order houses, retailers, and trade outlets catering to interior designers and architects. When searching for tableware, don't neglect sources of designs of the past: antiques shops; companies specializing in discontinued china, silver, and crystal patterns; secondhand shops; flea markets; and bargain stores—these are all wonderful places to hunt for the imaginative designs of yesteryear.

In the end, *Dining in Style* is a book of ideas, not rules. It is a guide to the many products available on the market and suggests ways to combine them to achieve the look you want. When read with care, it will inspire you to view setting the table in a new light, not as a last-minute chore before guests arrive but as an enjoyable and fulfilling pastime.

Center: *A contemporary black-and-white color scheme punctuated by vibrant red accents unifies a sophisticated selection of table basics—dinnerware, flatware, serving pieces, and accessories.* **Right, top to bottom:** *The range of choices has never been wider from informal, yet sleek, interlocking picnic flatware and casual cotton place mats to glittering glassware that can be combined into either an elaborate dinner setting or a simple dessert service.*

THE ELEMENTS

Practically every table setting consists of the same basics—flatware, dinnerware, glassware, serving pieces, a centerpiece, and decorative accessories. Within these broad categories, however, is a wide variety of products from which to choose. To see what types of items are available, it's necessary to look at each category individually.

Flatware

THE TERM "FLATWARE" IS GENERALLY APPLIED TO eating utensils. Because they are the most durable element of any table setting, flatware pieces are usually chosen first, before dinnerware and glassware. The classic choice for flatware is sterling silver, but there are others that work equally well: silver plate, stainless steel, and even gold.

Use of the term "sterling silver" is set by law and professional standards. To be labelled sterling, the silverware must be composed of a ratio of 925 parts pure silver to 75 parts of a base metal, which strengthens the piece. Though the proportion is set by law and custom, the weight of sterling-silver flatware varies greatly. Heavier pieces contain more silver and, therefore, are more expensive. Major manufacturers include such well-known names as Gorham, Kirk, Reed & Barton, Towle Silversmiths, Wallace-International, and Georg Jensen.

While there are many sterling-silver patterns, they fall into a few general groupings: Colonial, baroque, and contemporary. The sleek sculptural lines of the latter are sometimes embellished with naturalistic detailing to soften its visual impact. Generally, sterling-silver flatware is sold in six-piece place settings consisting of a fork, knife, salad fork, butter knife, soup spoon, and teaspoon. This initial set can be augmented with any number of supplementary pieces ranging from cocktail forks to spoons for salt dishes, fruit, and iced beverages to fish forks and knives.

Silver plate originated in Sheffield, England, in the early eighteenth century. Its impact was profound and spurred the rise of an entirely new industry. Whereas silver flat-

Left: *Sterling-silver flatware patterns range from the contemporary to the traditional. The glory of baroque design is reflected in the sterling-silver serving pieces that will complement a traditional formal dinner setting.*

ware traditionally had been limited to the wealthy, silver plating made it available to many more people. Sheffield plate, as the ware is called, was created by coating a core composed of a nonprecious metal with a layer of silver. Today, this process is accomplished by a complex chemical reaction called electroplating.

Like sterling, silver plate varies in its weight depending on the amount of silver it contains. For added durability silver plate is often reinforced with additional silver where it receives the most wear, such as the backs of forks that are laid on the table surface.

Decorating silver adds to its luster and visual appeal. One of the most common methods is *chasing,* or cutting a design into the silver with a very sharp tool. *Engraving* involves cutting a design such as the owners' initials, or monogram, into the flatware. *Embossing* is a raised design and is commonly the decoration of choice for borders on serving pieces. *Repoussé* is another raised design created by pounding the flatware from the underside with tiny hammers.

Both sterling silver and silver plate are finished in one of three ways: bright or highly polished, matte or dull, or with a twill-like effect called Florentine.

The experts insist that the best way to keep your silver shining is simply to use it every day. This practice prevents the buildup of tarnish resulting from the chemical reaction that occurs when silver is exposed to the air. Keep silver away from foods and materials such as rubber, newspaper, salt, and vinegar that will cause an adverse chemical effect.

For sheer elegance nothing beats the look of vermeil, or gold flatware. Actually, vermeil is sterling silver that has been plated with a layer of gold. Vermeil is available in many of the same patterns as sterling silver. In addition, it can be decorated by the same methods. Unlike silver, however, vermeil flatware will not tarnish.

One of the most significant developments in flatware is stainless steel, a material that grew out of World War II. Quality stainless steel is impervious to staining by the chemicals in food. It is also dishwasher-safe, extremely long lasting, and inexpensive, especially compared to sterling silver and vermeil.

In the past, stainless steel was manufactured primarily in contemporary patterns. Now, the scope has been widened to encompass Colonial and even baroque designs, which has expanded stainless-steel flatware's market appeal. Generally, stainless-steel flatware is sold as a five-piece set with a fork, knife, teaspoon, salad fork, and soup spoon.

This array of sterling-silver flatware includes almost everything needed for the table. **Top row, left to right:** *A knife for fruit or cheese, luncheon knives, a dinner knife, two teaspoons and a soup spoon, dessert fork, salad fork, dinner forks, and an iced teaspoon are the basics.* **Second row:** *Serving spoons are shaped to accommodate virtually any food you prepare. Shown left to right are two large serving spoons for vegetables, a ladle for gravy or sauce, a spoon for nuts, and a jelly spoon.* **Third row:** *The cake knife is distinguished by its wide blade for easy serving; the salt spoon by its small, deep bowl; the two butter knives for the serving plate by their short, wide blades with the pointed tips; and the butter knives for individual place settings by their short, blunt blades. A smaller version of a dinner fork, knife, and teaspoon is made by most manufacturers for children. The tongs are made to grip cubes of sugar.* **Bottom row:** *Extras for your flatware set include a fork for condiments, two types of jelly spoon, a fork and spoon for a small child, an iced teaspoon, and pickle and relish forks.*

Dinnerware

EXCEPT FOR GLASS AND PLASTIC, THE DINNERWARE we eat off is ceramic. There are several steps in manufacturing this ware. First, a mixture of various clays is shaped by machine or by hand on a potter's wheel. After it is fired, or baked, in a kiln, the piece is decorated and coated with a glaze that protects the piece while giving it either a bright or dull appearance. Next, the ware is returned to the kiln to be baked again. Ceramics vary widely depending on the types of clays used, the temperature at which they are baked, and the level of craftsmanship involved in their creation.

◆ CHINA ◆

The most widely known form of ceramic dinnerware is china, as it is called in the United States and Great Britain, or on the continent, porcelain. Though we tend to think of china as a fragile material, it is surprisingly tough and durable. Much of our erroneous impression stems from the fact that china is strong enough to be crafted into exceptionally thin, delicate-looking plates and cups. Another reason is that china is translucent. You can hold a piece of china dinnerware up to the light and see the shadow of your hand through the material. This characteristic makes it easy to differentiate china from other types of ceramic dinnerware. In addition, china, like crystal, will ring when lightly tapped. And it is vitrified, which simply means it is smooth like glass and not porous or absorbent.

There are several varieties of china. In Great Britain bits of bone or bone ash are added to the clay mixture to create the exceptionally white product called bone

Left: *Typical of patterns that will strike a traditional tone on your table, this pattern is enlivened by the richness of gold. The luster of gold—coupled with a beautiful deep blue—forms a complex pattern that firmly establishes a contemporary atmosphere with traditional overtones.*

china. It is made by most British manufacturers including Minton, Royal Crown Derby, Royal Doulton, and Wedgwood.

Well-known makers of china in the United States include Lenox, Robert Haviland & C. Parlon, Salem China Company, and Mottahedeh. The major continental porcelain companies include Louis Lourioux in France, Robert Ginori in Italy, Rosenthal and Arzberg in West Germany, and Royal Copenhagen in Scandinavia. Many of these companies have extensive operations around the world.

Because china is vitrified, it will not absorb food particles that provide a comfortable breeding ground for germs. As a result, commercial grades of china traditionally have been used by hotels and restaurants. Strictly utilitarian in nature, this type of china is made the same way as fine china but is heavier in weight and thicker for even better durability.

The recent rise in popularity of the industrial style is evidenced by the many consumers who favor the clunky cups and plates associated with eating in a diner for use in their own homes. Thus a new product line was developed for the consumer market called casual china. Designed for everyday use, casual china is fabricated in the same way as the commercial ware but is lighter. Trend Pacific of Japan manufactures a lovely all-white casual china pattern called ''Basic V.'' Other interesting imported ca-

sual china comes from Artex and Alfol di Porcelains in Hungary.

Some brands of china, including the most delicate-looking, are made with sufficient flame and heat resistance that they can be used for cooking or baking. To achieve this strength, the Louis Lourioux concern bakes its porcelains at fourteen hundred degrees centigrade.

A basic place setting of china consists of five pieces: a dinner plate, salad plate or bowl, bread-and-butter plate, a cup, and a saucer. Some patterns are sold by the individual piece, others only in sets. In a new twist, Royal Doulton offers seven coordinated patterns in a program called ''designs à la carte'' that can be freely mixed to create a personalized look. These particular patterns come in two colors: dusty rose and blue. Most china place settings can be supplemented with any number of dishes in the same pattern. Some of the most popular include the luncheon plate, soup plate, cream-soup cup and stand (a two-handled, slightly footed soup cup), covered soup dish, lug (a two-handled soup dish), egg cups, individual salts, and assorted serving pieces.

Most fine china is dishwasher-safe although hand-painted pieces should be washed by hand to protect the decoration. When storing china, separate the plates with napkins or sheets of plastic. Better yet, store each piece in a plastic or cellophane cover and hang cups from individual hooks.

Left: *If your decorating preference is the country style, you won't go wrong by investing in a set of casual dinnerware awash with the colors of spring flowers.* **Right:** *Though designed early in this century, this Russian-inspired china pattern remains sufficiently radical in its appearance to set an avant-garde mood on your table.*

Above: Children's parties, casual breakfasts, and other informal occasions dictate dinnerware in bright, primary colors such as these designs manufactured for Marimekko and pictured on a complementary tablecloth.

Below: Besides durability, ironstone offers another advantage—beauty. This lovely ware is fabricated in classically inspired shapes and decorated with colorful floral motifs.

◆ STONEWARE ◆

Like china, stoneware is vitrified and strong. However, it is opaque, much less refined and elegant in appearance, and is imbued with a casual air that is thoroughly in keeping with informal dining. Marimekko makes a beautiful line of undecorated white stoneware while Bennington Potters in Vermont is well known for its stoneware decorated with two layers of glazing that give these pieces an enticing mottled appearance. Wedgwood in Great Britain makes a beautiful stoneware pattern called ''Stonehenge White.'' Designed by Roy Midwinter in the early 1970s, it is bold and sculptural in appearance. ''Stonehenge White'' is considered by many art historians to be one of the best contemporary ceramic designs.

Left: *An outstanding example of contemporary design is Roy Midwinter's pattern for Wedgwood. Besides its bold beauty, this stoneware offers another advantage—the serving pieces double as bakeware.*

Above: *Creative design has brought earthenware to new heights of sophistication—and consumer appeal. The eye-catching decoration on this terracotta dinnerware is created by leaving portions of the base exposed and adorning the remaining area with colorful glazes in bold designs.*
Below: *A bright pattern in yellow and blue with a straightforward star design in the center is typical of modern work in earthenware.*

◆ EARTHENWARE ◆

Although the term "earthenware" may conjure up images of inexpensive terracotta pottery, it encompasses much more. Earthenware incorporates many of the same ingredients as china. It differs, however, because the temperature at which it is baked is lower and the manufacturing process simpler. As a result, earthenware usually is much less expensive.

There are other differences, too. Unlike china, earthenware is opaque. It is not vitrified so it is not as strong. However, because

Far left: *A bouquet of subdued colors and an intricate latticework pattern around the rim decorate a more traditional design.*
Above: *This lively earthenware pattern with a fruit motif is perfect for a cozy supper of soup or stew.*
Below: *Two terracotta designs—one emblazoned with stripes, the other with intricate latticework—blend seamlessly.*

earthenware is baked at a lower temperature than china, it retains color decoration better. This may be an important factor in your selection of dinnerware if you prefer vibrant colors.

Earthenware is made in almost every style from historically inspired patterns to the highly contemporary. And it includes many varieties: ironstone, an extremely strong ware, and majolica, the colorful ceramic created in seventeenth-century Spain. Many individual craftspeople work in earthenware.

Left: *One of the most pleasing developments in tableware is a new emphasis on a long-ignored area—plastic. Attuned to trends in the home-furnishings market, product designers have enlivened this inherently light material with fashion colors and decorative effects including marbling.*

Right: *Glass dinnerware is rich in design tradition as the Aalto dinnerware clearly demonstrates. Designed in 1932 by Finnish architect Alvar Aalto, the pressed-glass pattern is enlivened by stepped rings. Accompanying flatware is designed by Achille Castiglioni.*

◆ GLASS AND PLASTIC ◆

The number of glass dinnerware manufacturers is more limited than for china, stoneware, or earthenware. However, the products available are quite striking and exciting and are guaranteed to satisfy the table designer's need for diversity and creativity. Anchor Hocking makes transparent dinnerware with a raised pattern while Viking Glass is known for its rich colors including red, green, blue, and even black. The clear glass dinnerware made by Arcoroc in France is widely available at department stores and specialty shops. The company's product line is quite extensive with plates in both luncheon and dinner sizes. These pieces can be used by themselves or as liners for other service plates.

Corning Glass Works manufactures Pyro-Ceram, an opaque glass dinnerware that is sold to consumers in two patterns: "Corelle" and "Cornerstone." "Corelle" is available in white and in tinted colors; "Cornerstone" is manufactured only in tinted colors. Both are dishwasher-safe and, except for the cups, can be placed in a microwave oven. A clear glass dinnerware product by Corning, Pyrex Commercial, is sold on the consumer market in Great Britain.

All glass dinnerware is inherently vitrified and extremely durable.

Most plastic dinnerware is made with a lightweight but tough material called melamine, which is heated to a high temperature and molded into the desired shape. Many people think of plastic dinnerware as appropriate only for picnics and children's parties, but a renewed interest in fine design currently enlivening the entire home furnishings field has left its mark on plastic dinnerware, too. One of the most beautiful lines is Heller Designs' boldly contemporary "Hellerware," which comes in an array of rich, primary colors including deep blue, bright red, classic white, and sprightly yellow.

Most plastic pieces can be safely washed in a dishwasher, if they are placed on the top rack away from direct heat. Cleaning with abrasive cleaners is not recommended as the pieces can be scratched and the finish dulled.

In traditional surroundings—a place setting consisting of an Imari-inspired plate, sterling-silver flatware, and crystal—a glass serving plate adds a zestful contemporary character.

Handblown wine glasses and pressed-glass candleholders are perfectly compatible in a glittering traditional setting.

Glassware

NOTHING SETS THE MOOD FOR AN ELEGANT EVENING like glittering glassware. Whether your needs call for delicate crystal stemware or practical tumblers from the bar, you're certain to find exactly what you need in today's diverse market.

Left: *This setting shows two varieties of wine glasses and a water goblet for elegant dining. Whether they are lime glass or lead crystal, the effect is stunning with the brightly colored china, simple linen tablecloth, and neatly folded napkin.*
Right: *Lead crystal takes flight to artistic heights in a fluted champagne glass.*

♦ HOW GLASS IS MADE ♦

All glass is composed of the same raw materials: sand supplemented with soda, potash, lime, arsenic, and manganese, which are melted together in a hot furnace.

One of the oldest ways of shaping glass is by hand blowing. The art of *handblown glass* was developed around the beginning of the first century A.D. in Syria. Some of the most beautiful glassware is still fabricated this way, individually blown into a mold by a trained craftsperson to create a unique glass object.

Pressed glass is an American invention dating from 1827. It is made by pouring liquid glass into a mold where it is evenly distributed by a plunger. Once the glass has solidified, the plunger is withdrawn, leaving a smooth, evenly formed interior surface.

These two methods of glassmaking come together in some brands of stemware in which the bowl is handblown and the base pressed. More expensive stemware has a base of cut crystal.

Handblown glass is light and delicate in appearance. Individual pieces will vary slightly in their height or thickness. Pressed glass is heavier and is more casual and uniform in appearance. Though there are many ways to categorize glassware for the home, the most straightforward is to divide the subject into two categories: clear and colored.

A trio of classic, modern glassware designs are grouped together. From left: the three sizes of the 1937 "Savoy" vase by Alvar Aalto, manufactured in Finland by iittala; the 1977 "Dyonisos" decanter by Van Day Truex made in France by Baccarat; the "Aarne" champagne glasses designed by Goran Hongell in 1948 and made in Finland by iittala. Because of their purity of form and exacting craftsmanship, these pieces have been honored by being selected for many museum collections.

◆ CLEAR ◆

The term "crystal" usually refers to *lead crystal,* while clear, plain glassware is known as *lime glass.* As a general rule lead crystal is used for more formal occasions while lime glass is the most common form of glassware for informal dining and everyday use. Lead crystal is defined by law as glassware that is composed of at least twenty-four percent lead oxide; lime glass is lead-free. Lead oxide is what gives lead crystal its remarkable clarity and sparkle. It also increases the strength of the glassware. The age-old test to determine if a glass is lead crystal is to tap it lightly; a lead-crystal glass will ring. However, be aware that this test is not as reliable as it may seem at first; almost any glass shaped like a bell rings when struck. If you cannot readily determine whether a glass is lime glass or lead crystal, ask the salesperson.

Well-known manufacturers of crystal include Towle in the United States, Waterford in Ireland, Orrefors in Sweden, Saint Louis, Lalique, and Baccarat in France.

On the table, clear lead crystal adds sparkle and enhances the formality of fine china, gleaming silver, and elegant linens.

Two varieties of wine glasses—cameo glass in green, amber, and blue; others with solid green stems—create spots of sparkling color on a transparent tabletop.

♦ COLORED ♦

This variety of glassware can be transparent like crystal or opaque as in milk glass. In transparent glass, the tint is created by adding chemicals into the mixture when the raw materials are melted. Because the color becomes fused into the glass, it will not fade over time. Colored glass is made in a range of patterns, which makes it suitable for elegant or casual dining.

Nontransparent glass encompasses two general types. *Milk glass* is opaque, a result of the whiteness of the basic chemical mixture. Similar to milk glass is *opaline,* which is somewhat transparent. Both are particularly suitable when devising a table setting that is imbued with the country spirit.

Viewing this beautiful selection of glassware, it's easy to understand why barware and stemware blend so effectively on the table. From left, the grouping encompasses three glasses for red wine, two fluted champagne glasses (at rear), a water goblet (at center), a glass for white wine, and an all-purpose balloon-shaped wine glass.

♦ STEMWARE AND BARWARE ♦

Glassware also can be organized descriptively as either stemware or barware. Stemware consists of a bowl set on a stem. It is considered more formal than barware although many stemware patterns are informal. Generally, stemware sets include a goblet, various sizes of wine glasses, a sherbet dish that doubles as a champagne glass, a cocktail glass, and a cordial.

Traditionally, the term ''barware'' refers to glasses for serving alcoholic drinks. Many of these glasses, however, are used for informal dining. For example, large highball glasses often hold iced tea and other cold summer beverages. While tumblers are usually associated with the serving of highballs, they also hold many other types of drinks such as milk and water. One of the most popular bar glasses is the old-fashioned, a short tumbler. It is a favorite of people who like their drinks on-the-rocks or who want a big serving of fruit juice at breakfast. In vogue today is the double old-fashioned, which holds a few more ounces.

Besides these three basics, there are many other types of barware—the slender Pilsner glass and broad mug, both for beer; the brandy inhaler or snifter; the sherry glass; and the saucer-shaped, hollow-stem, and tulip-shaped champagne glasses.

Decorative effects imbue glassware with a unique mood. An air of formality is instantly created by the Lalique "Vase Bacchantes," which is reminiscent of Renaissance sculpture.

Far left: *Whimsical barware (above) invites guests to lift anchor for a good time at a poolside party. Tumblers decorated with stars (below) form their own amusing constellation and suggest an excellent way to start the day with breakfast fruit juice.*
Left: *"Bristol" crystal by Saint Louis will complement a classic table setting.*

◆ SPECIAL EFFECTS ◆

Glassware can be decorated in any number of ways. *Cut glass* usually has a strong design that has been literally carved into the surface, most often by hand. Glass can also be etched with either acid or sand to create the impression that an artist has "drawn" a decorative pattern with a knife. An effect similar to etching results when a craftsperson utilizes a small copper wheel to create *engraved glass*.

Still another decorative table element is *hand-painted glass*. This type of ware should be washed individually to protect the decorative finish. A frosted effect results when a finished glass is dipped into an acid bath, which creates what is called *satin glass*. One of the most elaborate decorative effects is called casing, resulting in what is historically known as *cameo glass*. To create this outstanding glassware, one layer of clear or white glass is covered with a second layer of colored glass. To further enhance the visual effect, portions of the outer layer can be cut away to form a decorative pattern of contrasting colors in deep relief—a striking effect for the table.

Serving Pieces

BESIDES BEING INTRINSICALLY PRACTICAL, SERVING pieces for the table help to visually unify the setting. If you select serving pieces in the same pattern as your china service, the look will be uniform; contrasting serving pieces will give the table a zestful air.

The variety of ceramic serving pieces has been broadened considerably in recent years with the development of china that doubles as bakeware. Louis Lourioux, the French porcelain firm, includes in many of its patterns matching bakeware such as casserole dishes, ramekins, and pans for tarts and quiches. Hall China manufactures a streamlined white china baking dish suitable for the table.

The informal look of earthenware plates is greatly enhanced with stoneware cooking and serving pieces. Manufacturers now make cooking pieces that are suitable for use on the table; look for pieces that are oven-, microwave-, and dishwasher-safe. Some may come with matching platters

Left: *What hostess wouldn't want to hook these platters for serving the gifts of the sea or the local lake? Some of these lovely ceramic pieces are large enough for serving large groups while the smaller plates are appropriate for serving individual appetizers at a cocktail party.*

to protect the surface of the table when serving.

Another serving item is the soup tureen. This essential piece is available in many ceramic dinnerware patterns from major manufacturers, including Villeroy & Boch. Soup tureens ease serving at the table and can also double as centerpieces.

Craft items strike a note of individuality on your table. Beautiful ceramic pieces are available in a variety of motifs including Eigen Arts' playful ceramic pumpkin casserole dish, platters by Beth Forer, and hand-painted platters by Beth Kaplan for ZIBA Designs.

The term *hollowware* is applied to serving pieces made of sterling silver and silver plate. Because sterling hollowware is extremely expensive, many people limit these pieces to smaller items: bonbon dishes, compotes, and salt and pepper shakers. These items can be supplemented by silver plate vegetable dishes, casseroles, chafing dishes, bowls, and pitchers.

Multicolored yet subtly blended linens woven to resemble hopsacking bring a welcome sense of texture—and informality—to the table.

Linens

ONCE YOU HAVE CHOSEN THE BASIC ELEMENTS OF your table setting, now is the time to evoke the mood you want with table linens. If you prefer the aura of elegance, you might want to select lace to complement your finest china. For a country feeling, choose small floral designs. By contrast, large floral patterns will imbue your table with a sense of romance, and simple plaid designs will complement casual china and earthenware.

You can heighten the mood you want to create with different types of linens—tablecloths, napkins, placemats, and runners—for the center of the table. They can be used individually or combined innovatively to make your table the center of attention in the room.

Actually, the term "linens" is a misnomer, as textiles for the table are made in a range of materials. Although linen and lace are the classic choices, there are cotton, easy-care blends of polyester and natural fabrics, and more exotic fibers such as pineapple. These textiles can be complemented by crocheted and embroidered borders that recall the painstaking handiwork of the past.

Many substitutes for table linens aren't textiles at all. Rattan placemats are popular for casual dining; solid sheets of mirror and chrome will add a surprising touch of glitz to a table setting.

With table linens, you can also indulge in the beauty of contemporary handicrafts. Or scour flea markets and attend house sales to collect antique linens to give your table a one-of-a-kind look. Though many of these tablecloths will be damaged by stains or have deteriorated from age, these portions can be camouflaged with overlays. If the material is extensively damaged, you can recycle it to make napkins that are distinctive and beautiful. Because of a resurgence in historic textile designs, a number of fabric houses offer new reproduction products that coordinate with antique tableware and traditional decorating schemes.

Centerpieces

EVERY TABLE SETTING NEEDS A FOCAL POINT, AND almost always that element is the centerpiece. When asked what makes the best centerpiece, interior designers invariably opt for flowers. It's easy to understand why. Flowers bring color, texture, and a sense of delicacy to the table that cannot be matched by any other type of centerpiece.

The simplest approach to designing a floral centerpiece is to arrange cut flowers loosely in a vase. The experts recommend low centerpieces with flowers that fall away to the sides such as freesia or tulips rather than those that stand upright and block the view across the table. As an alternative many hosts or hostesses float a single, large flower blossom in a crystal bowl. A freshly cut magnolia blossom is exactly the right size and will add a fragrance to the dinner setting that is sweet but will not overpower perfume or cologne.

For casual yet stylish settings, the floral centerpiece can be presented in straw or rattan baskets. Arrange white lilacs, grape hyacinths, pale roses, and azaleas in a pretty hand-dyed twig basket or group fragrant flowers in a low, country-style basket. This arrangement can be embellished with fresh strawberries so that guests can literally nibble at the centerpiece. Another idea for an edible centerpiece is to fill a wooden cheese crate with carefully placed moss and trailing ivy studded with flowering branches and blue hydrangeas. Add to that a serving of cheese and pâté on a bed of black grapes, and your centerpiece is as delectable as the meal you serve.

For more permanent centerpieces, small, live plants make perfect arrangements. Buy preplanted seedlings of various seasonal flowers, such as the ever-appropriate lily of the valley. Planting the seeds in a decorated delft pot makes for a beautiful yet extremely practical centerpiece; all you do is water it

and wait about four weeks for the flowers to blossom.

Topiary—the art of trimming trees or shrubs into ornamental shapes—is enjoying a strong resurgence in popularity, and small-scale versions are perfect as centerpieces. Shaped into any number of motifs, these centerpieces also will become the focus of dinner conversation. Inventive topiary designs of ivy suitable for the table (or fireplace mantel) are sold by many stores and through mail-order sources.

People who want to decorate with floral centerpieces in the middle of winter also have the option of buying artificial flowers. Shunned in the past for their plastic, artless look, artificial flowers made today are much more natural in appearance. In addition, the selection has widened to include larger, more exotic flowers in popular colors like mauve, blue, peach, and coral. You can buy artificial flowers individually and arrange them yourself or many florists and specialty

shops will arrange them for you. Large-scale artificial flowers in a sleek contemporary-styled container are particularly popular.

There are other alternatives to the floral centerpiece. Fruits and nuts combined in a bowl make a festive, lovely centerpiece. If you're enjoying an oceanside vacation at a beach house, collect seashells, sand, and interestingly shaped stones to make a centerpiece ideally suited to the surroundings. The sand can be placed in silver-lined paper running the length of the table and decorated with the shells and stones. For entertaining in the country, stylist Kim Freeman suggests cutting small evergreen branches and dotting them with pine cones and small votive candles. The advantage of these centerpieces is that they cost practically nothing. Collecting the various elements becomes a fun group project and gives every person an opportunity to exercise his or her creativity.

Left: *An inventive idea for table setting is to arrange an undulating string of candles down the table and have the centerpiece also serve as lighting.* **Right:** *The low profile of a single gardenia blossom lends a sense of high style to an inviting breakfast setting. In wintertime when flowers are scarce and expensive, many hostesses opt for a nonfloral centerpiece.*

Decorative Effects

ACCESSORIES ARE THE FINISHING TOUCHES THAT IMbue the table setting with your unique personality. These decorative effects range from vases, candlesticks, and salt and pepper shakers, to baskets, bowls, and napkin rings. The materials from which to choose are just as varied. Your selection will depend on the mood you wish to evoke and the compatibility of the accessories with your dinnerware, glassware, and flatware.

The standard flower container, the vase, is made in a variety of materials including crystal, art glass, china, and other ceramics such as terra-cotta. One of the most beautiful pieces ever designed is the Modern classic ''Savoy'' vase by Alvar Aalto. Consisting of clear crystal in a swirling, organic shape, it is as appropriate today as it was when the great Finnish architect designed it for the Savoy Restaurant in Helsinki in 1937. There are several sizes but one of the most popular is 6¼ inches high made by iittala. Another timeless clear crystal vase that has inspired many variations is the ''Ovalis,'' a 10-inch high masterpiece designed in 1958 by Rapio Wirkkala.

Craftswoman Nancee Meeker fabricates a sculptural porcelain vase with a richly detailed crackle glaze. In sharp contrast are the contemporary vases by Jenkins Ceramics Manufacturing Company. These vases are available on the retail market in a wide range of colors and finishes. Small, 3⅞-inch terra-cotta vases by other manufacturers are sold by Conrans.

Because glass candlesticks add a sense of sparkling elegance to fine china and silver, they are another decorative accessory that will enhance any table setting. Today,

Artfully grouped on a sideboard, a frosted glass compote and a crystal ice bucket are evocative of a still-life painting.

reproductions of nineteenth-century originals in the shape of dolphins and other fanciful creatures are available. Though made of china, the candlesticks designed by Kitty Bright for Fresh Fields evoke an unmistakably country air with their low base, simple shape, and restrained decoration. For a rustic feeling of a different sort, look for inexpensive wood candlesticks. And to brighten your outdoor table settings, add a pair of hurricane lamps with delicate glass globes and copper bases.

The popularity of woven baskets continues unabated. Versatile enough to hold a central flower arrangement or carry a picnic meal to the beach, they are made in a number of sizes. A coil basket is an excellent container for fruit on casually set tables, while hand-dyed baskets hold breads and wrapped flatware for an outdoor buffet. Some of the most unusual and rare baskets are those made of woven pine needles.

In general, the new attention being given to decorative accessories is evidenced by the wide variety of well-designed tabletop goods currently on the market. These pieces include inexpensive and funky pastel ceramic coasters, starkly contemporary salt and pepper shakers, and opulent sterling silver salt and pepper shakers with caps made of pricey materials such as vermeil. Many of the more expensive items are sold only at specialty shops, while less expensive yet aesthetically pleasing and functional items can be purchased at most department stores.

Center: *The opulence of this formal table setting is matched only by the elegant dining room in which it is laid. The glittering crystal glassware mirrors the beauty of the candleholders and the chandelier overhead. To add a touch of whimsical, unforgettable elegance the household staff has fluffed the napkins into towering peaks.* **Right, top to bottom:** *From a lovely outdoor luncheon to an impressive array of fruit, bread, and cheese for a party to the sheer fun of the pattern on the paper dinnerware set, less formal occasions, too, can reflect a sense of care and attention to detail.*

FROM INFORMAL TO HAUT SETTINGS

Just as there are appropriate clothes for a variety of social occasions, there are different ways to dress up a table. You wouldn't wear a bathing suit to a business luncheon or a three-piece suit to the beach. Nor would you select paper plates for an elegant or romantic dinner or fine china for a beach party. Depending on the event, however, either choice is correct. Let's look at some table-setting ideas for both casual and more formal dining.

Paper and Plastic

GENERALLY, PAPER AND PLASTIC DINNERWARE AND accessories are associated with casual meals—garden barbecues, picnics in the woods, and afternoons at the beach. But as a result of new design and color options being offered today, plastic and paper products are now suitable for other adult gatherings. To reflect today's cultural phenomenon, you could, for example, host a "yuppie" buffet party with argyle-printed paper plates and chic plastic champagne glasses.

The easiest way to create your own table setting with plastic and paper is simply to buy a prepackaged set. These usually include plates for both the entree and dessert, salad bowls, plastic flatware, tumblers, and napkins. Some sets come with trays that have a circular indentation in which the tumbler is placed for easy carrying. With a handy red tote bag with room to pack food, the set is complete.

Your table setting is certain to become the center of attention if you opt for a Memphis-like look. A design group based in Italy, Memphis is known for its stark architectural furniture and fabric designs in bright colors. American designer Georges Briard has created his own interpretation of this style with vibrantly colored square paper plates and napkins emblazoned with abstract designs. These can be placed on his lacquer-look plastic tray in black with turquoise trim or red with black trim. Supplement these with Briard's "Sunburst" ice bucket that is 7¼ inches square, and four matching glasses. To complete the picture, he designs square coasters that are available in sets of six.

The most fun, however, is combining indi-vidual pieces to create your own exciting table settings. The key with paper and plastic dinnerware is to coordinate the disparate materials with color. For example, choose all-white ware for a tailored effect. Contrasting plates, tablecloths, and glassware add visual variety to the table.

Manufacturers of housewares are taking heed of trends in the home-furnishings market and are now making their products in today's popular "fashion" colors—black, pinks, and purples—with special effects such as marbling. A striking table setting that is eminently practical for an afternoon at the beach is an all-black blend of octagonal- or oval-shaped plastic plates frequently sold in novelty stores. The oval plates also come in a dessert-sized version, all in white. Marimekko creates attractive black-and-white paper plates that have a black ground and a stylized white floral

which you place the tableware and are available in sets of four in red, blue, or black.

Lillian Vernon's sophisticated black plastic serving trays resemble lacquer work. These pieces are perfect for indoor entertaining. Many card shops also sell cardboard baskets about eighteen inches long that are charming and practical for serving bread and vegetables. One of the most fun items you can use for serving is a plasticized paper container exactly like the ones in which Chinese restaurants package takeout orders. Previously limited to the commercial restaurant market, they are now available to the public and are an excellent way to pack small picnic servings and snacks.

Plastic glassware has also taken on an entirely new, sophisticated look. Elegant six-ounce fluted champagne glasses made of acrylic are reusable, scratch-resistant, and can be cleaned in the dishwasher. Sold at department and gourmet stores, this glassware is not quite as refined as the real thing but infinitely more practical for informal settings like a picnic. Clear plastic champagne glasses are also decorated with a number of irreverent designs, including a tuxedo bow tie near the top of the glass. For a different look, beautiful, silver-colored plastic tumblers are readily available in many party-supply and convenience stores.

Contrast paper and plastic tableware with natural accessories for a visually complete setting. At the beach, arrange candles in a mound of sand or place them on a piece of driftwood dotted with seashells or pebbles. Feel free to mix paper with plastic. Plastic plates and bowls are better suited for wet foods such as salads and entrees that are accompanied by sauces. For drier foods like cake, paper plates are sufficient.

Plastic dinnerware in deep, saturated blues and greens is perfect for the beach, especially when paired by stylist Kim Freeman with a woven basket and cloth in bright primary colors.

design. Coordinated napkins bear the same design in reverse—a black pattern on a white ground. Other napkins to look for in party stores are abstract zebra patterns in black and white, paper simulations of gray moiré, and paisley designs in muted colors.

Tablecloths come in black and clear plastic that will give your setting a sleek, chic look. For an elegant yet easily disposable decorative touch, embellish the cloth with white paper doilies and place mats. Longer-lasting plastic place mats are designed by Bobbi Bennis. Bordered with designs of dogs, chickens, and sheep, they are available at selected department stores. Some museum shops offer whimsical plastic place mats. They are shaped to follow the contour of an actual place setting with over-scaled outlines of a fork, plate, and knife on

Elegant Dining

THE FORMAL DINNER IS RELATIVELY RARE THESE DAYS. Nevertheless, it is well worthwhile to be familiar and comfortable with the formal table setting. Even if you host only casual dinner parties, you may someday be formally entertained and will need to know how a place setting is determined.

To arrange a formal place setting, put a salad plate to the left and above the service plate. Also situated to the left of the service plate are the napkin and forks for salad, the entree, and, sometimes, dessert. The dinner knife, teaspoon, and soup spoon are on the right of the service plate. Above them are the water goblet and, usually, two wine glasses, one for red, the other for white. There are no serving pieces as the guests are served individually at the table by the household help or the host couple. For the first course, a liner plate and a soup bowl should be placed on a service plate. After the first course these are removed and replaced with a dinner plate.

The formal dinner is the perfect opportunity to create a sparkling table setting of antique silver, crystal, and china. In fact, interior designer Gerrie Bremmerman of New Orleans, Louisiana, maintains that antique tableware is the secret of an enchanting table setting. It is not necessary, as it was in the past, that all the elements match. It is much more interesting when they don't as a rich blend of old silver, linens, and crystal evokes a special, individual style.

An excellent idea in this vein is to drape the dining table with an antique linen cloth on which is placed antique English earthenware plates, crystal water goblets, wine glasses, and antique sterling silver flatware.

For an eclectic touch, place a rustic wicker basket in the center of the table that is brimming with snapdragons, freesia, and abundant greens. Flank the centerpiece with tall white candles in crystal holders to complete an elegant table setting.

The formal table setting is as conducive to a relaxed and gracious dinner as the more casual place settings. As the host or hostess, you set the tone for the dinner—bringing individual servings to the table is one way to instill a more casual atmosphere. Carry plates into the dining area on trays that can then be stacked on a sideboard or serving table until it is time to clear the table. Doing this eliminates the need for elaborate serving pieces and reduces the amount of clutter on the table. Instead of a separate, formal dessert course, it is more fun to leave the table altogether and serve in the living room, study, or even outdoors on the terrace.

For an equally sophisticated but different setting, choose antique majolica dinner plates. If you like, substitute delicate handblown crystal tumblers for water goblets. Mix antique and new silver patterns. One wonderful combination of old and new that you can create is clean-lined late-Victorian silver mixed with Walter White's contemporary hand-hammered sterling flatware with handles shaped and decorated in an asparagus stalk motif. A modern flatware pattern in an antique design such as the "Queen Anne" pattern by Kirk Stieff is an excellent alternative to antique sterling.

In this sort of setting the centerpiece should be particularly prominent. A sterling silver or silver-plated water pitcher filled

The glory of gold creates the mood for this undeniably elegant setting. The subtle presence of the gold is carried through the vermeil flatware, the delicate rims of the crystal glasses, and through gold accents on the china. The centerpiece of red, white, and green strikes a colorful note on the otherwise monochromatic table.

Right: *In an elegant dining room it makes sense to arrange a table setting to match. Large service plates are flanked by sterling-silver flatware with the forks turned over and a formal arrangement of crystal. Lovely pink napkins arranged in the water goblets strike a festive note and complement the colors of the simple centerpiece.* **Center:** *Far more subtle is the low-key all-white theme. To enliven the setting, a textured tablecloth has been draped to the floor, and a vibrant green centerpiece is surrounded by four tall tapers.*

with colorful red or pink roses is the perfect addition. Because of the amount of silver in this table design, keep accessories minimal to avoid visual excess; limit them to small crystal bowls for salt and pepper with tiny silver spoons. A crisp white tablecloth draped to the floor provides a neutral background for the brightly colored majolica and gleaming silver.

Indulge in fancifully folded napkins. One

Left: *In an English dining room, the occasion takes on a more formal air with a pair of tall matching crystal candelabra. The green color scheme of the room is carried over to the table setting in the china. In a departure from tradition, napkins arranged in the dinner fold are placed on the salad plates.*

of the most popular folds for formal place settings is called the Astoria. It is folded so that the edges are tucked underneath and the center exposed. This fold is particularly appropriate for monogrammed napkins. Here's how to arrange the Astoria: first, fold the napkin into quarters with the free points at the bottom and the decoration face down on the table. Second, fold down the other corners. Turn the napkin over and the fold is complete.

Many other napkin arrangements work equally well on an elegantly set table. Some of these are the Chloe, fan, Algonquin, artichoke, bird of paradise, and bishop's hat. Instructions for these and many other folds are explained step-by-step in two very useful books, *Fancy Folds,* by Linda Hetzer and published by the Hearst Corporation in 1980, and *Folding Table Napkins*, published by Sterling Publishing Co., Inc. in 1972.

Friendly Kitchen Meals

HAVE YOU EVER NOTICED HOW GUESTS SEEM TO gravitate toward the kitchen? This room, more than any other in the house, stimulates memories from the past—of growing up, of warmth, of nourishment, and of love. Kitchen design has changed greatly since the days when this room was furnished with a counter or small tubular metal table suitable only for quick snacks or doing homework. Today, the kitchen often is a true living space geared for entertaining as well as food preparation. Besides the cooking facilities, work surfaces, and storage facilities you would expect to find, the modern kitchen frequently incorporates dining and sitting areas, and, sometimes, even a media center equipped with a television set and stereo components.

The kitchen is the nerve center for preparing meals, which makes dining here inherently casual. The meal may be a leisurely weekend breakfast for just the two of you, a casual family lunch or even a dinner for close friends who like to pitch in and help with the cooking. This arrangement frees the host or hostess to join in the before-dinner conversation rather than work alone while everyone else enjoys drinks in another room.

The key to a pleasingly decorated table is to keep the setting simple. At breakfast it may consist of nothing more than casual chinaware in white with a single band of color around the rim. This sort of ware is sold by many stores and kitchen shops under their own labels. A perfect example of a successful tabletop vignette is ceramic dinnerware imported from Italy matched with stainless-steel flatware in a restrained design. Flatware with acrylic handles inspired by the cutlery of French bistros is available at any number of retail outlets. This stainless-steel flatware is a classic yet reasonably priced element; it's perfect for your homey, casual setting.

Coordinate colors by selecting china with a blue band, flatware with blue handles, and for linens, napkins in a cotton-linen blend in a blue-and-white plaid pattern. Then for contrast, place several clay pots containing red geraniums on the table or breakfast bar as a colorful centerpiece.

This simple setting can be slightly modi-

fied for a casual lunch or family supper. For the bistro flatware, substitute a more ornate stainless-steel pattern like ''Paul Revere'' by Oneida or even sterling patterns including the stark, classically inspired flatware by Stanley Roberts of New York City. Instead of the cups and saucers you used at breakfast, select pressed-glass stemware by Libbey Glass, the manufacturing company in Toledo, Ohio. Solid-color cotton napkins in red or blue complete the setting and visually tie it together.

A dinner party for close friends is a perfect opportunity to create a more elaborate table setting. A wonderful idea in a rustic motif is to drape the table to the floor with contrasting under- and overcloths coordinated with napkins. To reinforce the country feeling, select wooden-handled flatware in the Scandinavian tradition and complete the look with earthenware dinner plates decorated with botanical motifs. Two or three old tin lanterns found at a local flea market will provide the low-level lighting that is desirable when dining. For a centerpiece, choose an old white crock pot and fill it with bright yellow daisies. Large wooden bowls and platters make excellent serving dishes and will complement the look of the wooden-handled flatware.

Of course, you can heighten the sense of elegance in the kitchen by adding as service plates drabware dinner plates—a khaki-colored china made by Wedgwood and other manufacturers. Then, in place of the wooden serving bowls, use old porcelain platters purchased from an antiques dealer. The platters need not match; in fact, the contrast of varied antique patterns will imbue the setting with a sense of the exotic. To punctuate this dramatic setting, look for sculptural crystal goblets.

Above: *A marble dining surface creates a more elegant setting for a kitchen meal. An interesting juxtaposition is the arrangement of an essentially simple dinner setting of china and crystal. The napkins on the dinner plates and the centerpiece hint at formality.* **Below:** *Breakfasting in the kitchen means getting down to basics in the form of primary colors. White china with blue decoration and blue-and-white plaid linens are exuberantly punctuated with red, tulips, and plastic-handled flatware and napkins that can only be described as "wake-up" yellow.*

This intimate outdoor brunch setting is an invitation to spend the afternoon enjoying good food and excellent company. The secrets? A glistening white cloth, pink-and-white china filled with beautiful fruits, champagne glasses, and a copy of the Sunday paper. On a nearby table, an unusual carved rabbit patiently ices the champagne.

Brunch on the Palazzo

NOTHING IS QUITE AS DELICIOUSLY DECADENT AS whiling away a Sunday afternoon at a stylish brunch. The occasion is even better if the setting is outdoors where the air is fresh, flowers are blooming, and the view is of a shimmering lake or an expansive, manicured lawn. The most practical way to set up your brunch on the palazzo—or terrace—is to divide the entire area into distinct zones with separate tables for dining and serving drinks. If you choose to offer a buffet brunch, set up a third table for serving food. Cover all the tables with cloths that fall to the ground to create a sense of elegance while camouflaging your everyday garden furniture. This approach is particularly effective on the bar table as it provides space to conceal practical, yet often mundane looking, plastic coolers containing wine, mixers, and extra ice.

Whether you decide to set up a buffet table or host a sit-down brunch, arrange dining tables for groups of four or six. If yours is a small gathering that requires only one table, you can streamline the entire affair by serving your guests from a dainty wicker trolley pulled directly up to the table.

Choose fabric with a small floral pattern on a pretty pastel background for a tablecloth to create the atmosphere of an English country garden. For a more formal background, select crisp white cotton or natural linen. Repeat the tablecloth fabric as napkins and as the upholstery on the chair cushions for a tailored setting.

A lovely china dinnerware perfect for an

elegant brunch on the terrace is the "Summer Palace" pattern from Royal Worcester Spode. This pattern consists of a white background with a center floral medallion in shades of blue. The dinner service will complement the beautiful "Kings" sterling-silver pattern from Georgian House Silversmiths with its ornately decorated handles. Complete the vignette with sculptural "Peer Gynt" water goblets and wine glasses in crystal from Hadeland of Norway.

For contrast, select accessories made of earthenware including individual salt cellars, a butter tub, and small ashtrays for guests who smoke. Beautiful earthenware accessories from France, where this ceramic is called faience, are versatile enough to be used in a number of different settings.

An outdoor brunch arranged as a buffet will ease your work as the host or hostess. Instead of continually having to check all of the dining tables to ensure that each has sufficient food, you can simply review the buffet table occasionally. This reduces the number of serving dishes you will need and minimizes additional trips to the kitchen.

Another stylish but more casual table setting can be created with earthenware plates and stainless-steel flatware rather than china and sterling. An excellent idea in dinnerware is the "Rosalyn" stoneware pattern designed by Carleton Varney and manufactured by International China. Couple this beautiful and durable ware with stainless-steel flatware in the "Grand Ribbon" pattern by WMF of America and crystal "Hampton" goblets by Sasaki. To add a spirit of elegance select antique accessories. These may be elaborately designed or simple wares such as lovely pressed-glass water pitchers and inexpensive, whimsical ceramic pieces.

Late-Night Candlelight Dining

WHAT COULD BE A BETTER WAY TO END AN EVENING after a concert or ballet than with a candlelight dinner? The feeling you want to evoke is a blend of opulence and romance using an abundance of candles and materials that bespeak the exotic. However, don't feel you have to rely on candlelight alone. If you have a chandelier hanging above the dining table the level of illumination can easily—and precisely—be set with the simple addition of a rheostat, or dimmer. For a candlelight dinner, the chandelier should be on the lowest possible setting giving off about twenty to forty watts of light.

The candles provide much more than light; they also establish the atmosphere. The easiest way to arrange them is to place large round candles in glass hurricane lamps flanking the centerpiece. A more imaginative idea, however, is to combine the lighting and the centerpiece. Fill a round cut-crystal bowl with water and float one large blossom in the center. (In a pinch, a clear glass soufflé dish will suffice.) One of the best flowers to use for this centerpiece is a magnolia, which adds beauty to the table and gives off a subtle fragrance. An excellent alternative is one large gardenia blossom. If the bowl is large enough add two or three small, buoyant votive candles. These ''floating candles,'' as they are called, will make the crystal bowl glow with a warm light, especially if it is embellished with facets.

Supplement this lighting scheme with a string of votive candles arranged in an un-dulating line so that they thread through the table setting. Be careful in placing the candles near serving pieces and glassware to ensure that a coat sleeve doesn't get caught in the flames. Additional candles placed around the dining room will reinforce the romantic feeling. These can be placed on any sideboard or serving cart or at other locations in the room that will be enhanced by a spot of flickering light. The candles will bathe the room in the right mood.

To imbue your everyday dining table with a sense of the exotic, stylist L.A. Clever of Houston suggests a setting in shades of purple, one of today's most popular colors in home furnishings. Instead of a traditional tablecloth, she drapes her dining table with a purple Indian sari accented by silver threads. On top of the sari you can place bone china dinnerware by Royal Doulton in one of its classic patterns: ''Carlyle,'' ''Harlow,'' or ''Carnation.'' To complete the setting leave a flower blossom on each dinner plate for your guest to wear.

An ornate sterling-silver pattern such as ''Grand Baroque'' made by Wallace-International or ''El Grandee'' by Towle Silversmiths will heighten the sense of opulence. Create contrast by adding glassware and accessories in the ''Manhattan'' Depression-glass pattern popular in the 1930s. Opaque and cut with facets that make it look like crystal, this glassware is just beginning to regain its popularity and is still plentiful in second-hand shops. With ''Manhattan's'' new-found popularity, how-

Asymetrically placed candles definitely set the mood for a romantic, late-night dinner for two. The pink-and-black color scheme is unusual—yet highly effective—in this setting.

ever, expect the cost to rise. If you prefer sleek contemporary stemware, substitute the beautiful Baccarat "Harcourt" pattern or Tiffany & Company's "Provence" crystal design. Crystal accessories with this motif will add a sense of clear brilliance to the table. Crystal candlesticks from the Swedish company Orrefors are also entirely appropriate.

Surrounded with this amount of luxury, tone the entire setting down by using men's simple, white handkerchiefs as napkins. A silver-plated tray makes an excellent serving piece to bring individual courses from the kitchen to the table and eliminates the need for other serving pieces. Place the tray on a sideboard until needed to return dishes to the kitchen.

Though envisaged for the dining room, the candle-lit table setting can just as easily be moved outdoors to the terrace or patio. In this case the candles should be protected from the breeze by glass hurricane lamps. Additional lamps or strings of tiny white lights can be interspersed in the shrubbery or among potted plants to create small pinpoints of illumination that will enhance the romantic atmosphere.

Center: *The most relaxed way to begin the day is by enjoying breakfast in bed. Here, a silver tray holds the essentials, all grouped compactly for easy carrying and elegant serving.* **Above right:** *A more traditional approach—and one perfect for a country-inspired kitchen or dining room decorating scheme— is utilizing simple stoneware. In this case, the selection is a striking white ware that is right at home on a rustic pine-plank table.* **Center right:** *Though a weekend lunch is an inherently casual affair, it need not be mundane maintenance for the body. To feed the soul, a midday meal has been moved outdoors where it can be enjoyed in simple sling chairs gathered around a table draped with a pretty pink cloth.* **Below right:** *A drapery wall forms a satiny background for a candle-lit dinner setting. Matching mats are the base of a simple place setting that is unified by the center runner. The tall candlesticks and the spare design of the floral centerpiece emphasize the understated elegance of this late-night setting.*

MORNING TO NIGHT, INSIDE AND OUT

You can almost tell the time of day by a quick look at the dining table. Early in the morning it will be set for breakfast with cereal bowls, tumblers for fruit juice, and the ever-present coffee cups and saucers. At midday on the weekend it may herald a festive lunch with simple pottery dinnerware and utilitarian stainless-steel flatware. Or perhaps you will join the infamous ''ladies who lunch'' and host a formal midday meal replete with special plates and sterling silver. In the late afternoon, you can also enjoy tea time, indulging in a light meal with a friend or neighbor.

Of course these meals are merely the prelude to dinner when the busy members of your family—or specially invited guests— come together for a relaxing evening of cocktails and a carefully planned meal, all punctuated with lively conversation that renews and strengthens the bonds of family and friendship. Each meal calls for a specific type of table setting to establish the proper mood and accommodate the foods you serve.

*Above: Breakfast in the kitchen need not mean a slice of toast taken hastily from the counter while reaching for the door. Take, for example, this eye-catching arrangement of pink, leaf-patterned ceramic ware on an extension of the work surface within easy reach of the range top. **Below:** The breakfast place setting is simple and practical. Around the plate and cereal bowl the other essentials of the bread-and-butter plate, flatware, and a coffee cup and saucer are placed for informal dining. The individual creamer and sugar container make the setting complete.*

Breakfast and Brunch

NUTRITIONISTS HAVE BEEN TELLING US FOR YEARS that breakfast is the most important meal of the day. Yet it creeps up on us unexpectedly every morning, getting lost in the rush to shower, shave, dress, and leave for work. Taking time for breakfast makes good sense. Physically, it gives you the energy to be creative and productive on the job. In an emotional sense, a festive table setting reinforces the benefits of breakfast by brightening the dreariest day and putting family members in an upbeat mood. The secret to creating this atmosphere is simple earthenware in sparkling white or bright colors. Or combine these two possibilities with a simple white tableware decorated with a colorful border around the rim. The best place to shop for this sort of ceramic is your favorite kitchen-specialty store.

Tumblers, reminiscent of jam or jelly jars, hold large servings of juice to start the day off on the right note. Beautiful tumblers in this vein are made by Saint-Gobain International Glassware Corporation in New York City. For a touch of elegance, serve your favorite morning juice in a fluted champagne glass or an all-purpose wine glass.

Breakfast is a perfect time to make things easy on yourself and select easy-care stainless-steel flatware that can be rinsed off and stored in the dishwasher until evening. Among the many lovely patterns available today is the "Modern Provincial" pattern by Reed & Barton of Taunton, Massachusetts. An eye-catching alternative is the "Palladio" pattern by Supreme Cut-

lery of Towle Silversmiths. This intriguing flatware is high-quality stainless steel with gold-plated accents on the handles.

The breakfast place setting is arranged with a small luncheon-sized plate in the center. Above and to the left of the plate is a bread-and-butter plate and a knife. The specific types of spoons and other flatware you will need vary depending on the menu. Generally, to the left of the plate is a fork and to the right, spoons for fruit and cereal as well as a knife. A variation is to place the cereal spoon at the top of the plate. The

coffee cup, saucer, and juice tumbler are positioned above the knife.

You need not buy specific serving pieces for a breakfast setting; indeed, your serving pieces can be part of your dinnerware service. If you prefer special serving pieces, visit second-hand and antiques shops for visually intriguing treasures such as nineteenth-century majolica cake stands to hold breakfast rolls or fresh fruit. Hand-crafted earthenware serving pieces in popular designs such as the fennel-shaped pitcher and serving bowl are ideal additions. Keep fresh breads and breakfast rolls warm by serving them wrapped in a colorful napkin tucked inside a woven basket. These

Breakfast for one is an event of solitary indulgence when enjoyed in a comfortable wicker chair at a table draped with a cloth to the floor in this bright sunroom. Atop the table, simplicity reigns in the subdued china, straightforward silver pattern, and wicker basket holding the fruit du jour.

pieces are stocked by many retail outlets ranging from your local grocery to plant stands and nurseries.

The foundation of your breakfast table setting is the table covering. Your options are nearly limitless. To imbue your table with Victorian elegance, select a lovely antique linen cloth with an embroidered or crocheted border. On a small table, a frilly pillow sham in a blend of polyester and cotton sets the same tone. Easier to care for are plasticized fabrics that can be cleaned by wiping with a damp cloth. These are offered by many textile companies in a range of patterns from quaint country prints to bold geometrics. If your table has beautiful wood graining, show it off by dispensing with a tablecloth altogether. Mark each place setting with a rattan or cloth place mat in natural earth tones.

Napkins can match the cloth and place mats or strike a note of contrast depending on your preference. For example, red napkins reinforce the monochromatic effect of a breakfast table set with red-and-white plates and a serving bowl filled with strawberries. Yellow napkins, on the other hand, add visual variety. You can purchase napkins individually or in coordinated sets. Better yet, make your own napkins with fabric remnants.

A basket filled with fresh flowers and lots of greenery is an excellent centerpiece that will perk up even the most determined laggard early in the morning. Make the centerpiece as colorful as possible by combining several varieties of flowers such as daisies, pansies, carnations, and sunflowers. If you have a garden, take the breakfast theme to an extreme and pick fresh morning glories. Or eliminate flowers entirely and fill a basket with fruit that family members can cut and add to their cereal bowls.

Because people are rushing off to school or the office in the morning, it is wise to keep the breakfast table setting simple during the week. On weekends and holidays, however, you can be a little more elaborate. Instead of placing coffee cups, saucers, and spoons at each individual place setting, group them together on a silver-plated tray by the hostess chair. This way, the hostess can serve each person his or her own cup of coffee or tea, thus giving others extra-personal attention.

If you entertain weekend guests frequently or are a member of one of those families in which everyone gets up at a different hour, a practical approach is to serve an English country breakfast. Arrange individual place settings on the table as you would during the week. Your job is easier, however, as serving dishes go on a sideboard or separate serving table so that people can help themselves. Fruit will look better—and stay fresh longer—when nestled in a bowl inserted in a larger container filled with ice. Fruit juice should be kept in a carafe, coffee in a vacuum jar. Keep food hot on a warming plate.

This type of arrangement is equally suited for serving brunch. However, the selection of food and drink should be wider. Supplement your offering of orange juice with tomato and grapefruit juice. A bottle of iced vodka set nearby will enable your guests to serve themselves a drink before eating. Contrast traditional scrambled eggs with a baked egg dish along with bacon, sausages, and potatoes. Round out your menu with a wide selection of interesting-looking breads, rolls, and muffins. A large coffee service and a carafe of hot water for tea complete the setting.

Lunch

DURING THE WEEK OUR CHOICE OF A MIDDAY MEAL seems terribly limited—it often consists of either a busy business gathering at a restaurant or, at the other extreme, a quick trip to the corner coffee shop or a sandwich eaten hastily at the desk. Unfortunately, many of us carry this hit-or-miss approach to eating lunch over to the weekend. Instead of relaxing over a leisurely midday meal, all too frequently we simply forage through the refrigerator for leftovers. The result is, at best, mundane.

There is a solution. Rather than settling for leftovers, treat yourself to a lunch of tasty cheeses, fresh fruit, interesting breads, and a dry white wine or wine spritzer. Serve them in a casual setting in the dining room most of the year. But in warm weather, make lunch a movable feast and eat outdoors on the terrace or in the garden under the shade of a large, old tree.

Indoors or out, drape the table to the floor with a cloth decorated with small-scale prints, geometric designs or narrow, colorful stripes. You can use matching napkins or create contrast by using thick white cotton arranged in a casual luncheon fold. To make this arrangement, fold the napkin into quarters with the free points at the top. Fold the right edge, then the left, over the center. Slip the napkin bottom-first through a napkin ring or secure it with a brightly colored ribbon. For added decoration insert a small flower blossom inside the holder.

Clear glass plates draw attention to the food. They look beautiful when used alone, more elegant if they are liner plates for exuberantly decorated service plates such as the enticing lavender-colored lacquered dinnerware made by craftsman Phillip Mueller.

White plates will also enhance the visual appeal of almost any food. Beautiful unadorned white ceramic dinnerware is made by Marimekko and Nuutajarvi Glass through Arabia of Finland in Niles, Illinois. Both have matching serving pieces and are sold at numerous retail outlets.

Carefree stainless steel is an eminently practical choice of flatware. A beautiful pattern is the "Sheraton" design by Oneida Silversmiths. Part of the Oneida Heirloom Collection, the "Sheraton" pattern is a stark contemporary design that has been visually softened by the addition of details including banding and decoration resembling engraving on the handles.

Your choice of glassware can vary greatly. If you prefer a glass of wine at lunch, enjoy it in a handblown crystal wine goblet. The selection from which to choose at retail is almost limitless. One of the most beautiful and inexpensive wine glasses is made by the German company Cristallerie Swiesel. This company's glassware is sold throughout the world. One of its most popular wares is called the banquet wine glass. For other beverages simple old-fashioned or double old-fashioned glasses will suffice quite nicely. These pieces can be bought in clear glass or in a range of colors including a lovely pale cranberry manufactured by Pilgrim Glass Corporation.

When several people gather, a simple lunch often becomes a more formal "luncheon." The occasion may be a regular meeting of friends, or be for a specific purpose.

Luncheon calls for a more elaborate table

setting. The traditional place setting consists of a luncheon plate and a soup bowl. To the left and above the plate are a bread-and-butter plate and a butter knife. To the left of the luncheon plate are the napkin and luncheon fork. On the other side of the plate are the luncheon knife, teaspoon, and soup spoon. Above these, place a water goblet and wine glass.

The best tablecloth for these occasions is a crisp linen with matching napkins in a subtle color. White is always in style as are off-whites like ecru and also soft pastels. Famous linen companies such as D. Porthault carry a bounty of lovely linens, many of which are decorated with intricately embroidered or scalloped borders. Napkins are arranged in the traditional luncheon fold, which is easy to master. Simply fold the napkin into quarters, then in half diagonally to form a triangle. Place the napkin to the left of the luncheon fork with the longest side of the triangle nearest the shaft.

Fine china sets the tone of the table. One of the loveliest varieties for a luncheon service is the ''Isabelle'' pattern from Bernaraud Porceleains de Limoges. This pattern has a thin band around the edge of the plate with a second, wreathlike border inside. In the very center of each plate is a colorful floral design.

Sterling silver adds to the sense of luxury and importance of the luncheon. Of the many fine sterling designs available today, one that is particularly appropriate for luncheon is the ''English Gadroon'' pattern by Gorham. Infused with the spirit of romance, this design has intricate and delicate detailing on the handles. To complete this picture-perfect setting, choose sculptural crystal wine glasses in the ''Allegro'' pattern by Lenox.

Above: *Lunch in the sunroom brightens anyone's day. The light and airy feeling of the outdoors is brought indoors via china decorated with flowers and matching place mats. The centerpiece injects a vivid spot of color while keeping a low profile so that conversation can flow freely across the table.* **Below:** *For a more formal occasion, china and tablecloths in shades of blue and white have been selected so as to reflect the colors of the dining room wallpaper.*

Tea

ANY DAY OF THE WEEK FROM ABOUT THREE TO FIVE o'clock in the afternoon is tea time. A hallowed tradition in Great Britain, taking tea is also becoming an American custom. With the relaxed atmosphere that surrounds tea time, it is easy to understand why enthusiasm for this great British tradition remains undiminished. Although seemingly outdated, sitting down to tea is an excellent way to entertain friends on a weekend afternoon. But tea doesn't require a crowd. It can just as easily be enjoyed by a couple or even alone. In warm weather you can move the tea service outside and relax in the sun.

Tea has a long and colorful history. As a result, there are many local variations throughout the British Isles. However, two are particularly popular: the traditional tea and the cream tea. The traditional approach is actually a light meal of thinly sliced watercress, cucumber, chicken, or tomato sandwiches followed by a tart or fruit cake. The cream tea is based on fresh scones, strawberry preserves, and whipped cream.

There is something particularly enjoyable about having a traditional tea in an equally traditional setting. Set the proper tone by serving from a mahogany tea trolley where trays for sandwiches, dessert trays, the dinnerware, flatware, linens and of course, the teapot are nestled. At tea time, serve from the trolley onto a mahogany table surrounded by small balloon-back ballroom chairs.

With a pretty table there is no need for a cloth; limit textiles to crisp, tailored linen napkins from Ireland. English china is perfect dinnerware for a traditional tea. Trish

Foley, an interior designer, editor, and author of a new book entitled *Having Tea,* suggests that you select cups, dessert plates, and a teapot of Wedgwood drabware.

Classically inspired flatware will reinforce the traditional spirit. An entirely appropriate choice is the "Ionic Supreme" sterling-silver cutlery manufactured by Towle Silversmiths. As the pattern name indicates, this flatware resembles an ancient column in its shape and is embellished with a small capital at the top of the handle.

Serve sandwiches from a round sterling-silver tray and place cakes on an antique silver cake stand. As a finishing touch, decorate each place setting with a pale pink rose in a sterling mint-julep cup as a substitute for a centerpiece.

A cream tea is completely compatible with a country decorating scheme—the single most popular design style for the past several years. Set the overall country tone with the food and teapot placed on a pine muffin stand. If you are entertaining a small group, arrange individual place settings. Larger groups are more efficiently served with the food and drink placed on the muffin stand as a minibuffet. Here is an excellent opportunity to enjoy using china with matching serving pieces in pretty floral designs on an all-white background. Punctuate the light and airy atmosphere created by your china with a white cotton tablecloth and napkins embroidered around the edges.

Unmatched antique sterling flatware looks wonderful in a table setting infused with the country spirit, and is an excellent way to use odd pieces found at flea markets and secondhand shops. Complete your country-inspired theme with a centerpiece consisting of a fig basket filled with lilies of the valley.

Above: *Any design will look especially enticing supplemented only by the food and a simple floral centerpiece on a round tea table.* **Below:** *Ceramic tea sets create a less formal ambience than do silver varieties. This one is rendered in white china with delicate floral detailing.*

Center: *In a
traditionally designed
dining room, the dinner
service and centerpiece
echo the eye-catching
colors of the upholstery.
To prevent the setting
from becoming too
excessive visually, light
transparent crystal was
chosen for the glassware
and candleholders. A
centerpiece flanked by
evenly matched groupings
of candles creates a
symmetrical core around
which individual place
settings have been
grouped.*

Dinner

THE FAVORITE MEAL OF THE DAY FOR MOST PEOPLE IS dinner. The workday is over and now is the time to relax and nourish the body with good food and the spirit with enjoyable conversation. For this occasion the dinnerware of choice is white china or earthenware, each of which brings a sense of formality to even the most casual table setting.

Many white wares are available in a variety of designs from informal to quite elegant. One of the loveliest—and an important ware in terms of fine design—is the trigger-handle ceramic made by Bennington Potters in Vermont. Featured in the collection of the Museum of Modern Art in New York City, it is sold at the museum's shop and by mail order. Very different, and very beautiful, white ware is manufactured by the Ralph Lauren Home Furnishings Collection.

Unabashedly country in feeling, antique yellowware is the perfect substitution to add the brilliance of color to the dinner setting. Bring in the atmosphere of the outdoors with ''Mon Jardin,'' a French earthenware by Longchamp. Or you can give your table a more formal air by selecting blue-and-white porcelain. This historic ware was first developed for the Chinese export market to Europe. Today, it is made by a number of manufacturers. Inexpensive ware of this type is sold at a variety of outlets. Authorized reproductions of museum-quality blue-and-white porcelains are manufactured by Mottahedeh.

As an added detail, place your dinnerware on wooden service plates or on rustic-looking teakwood plates. These can double as serving pieces for cheese and fruit and

Left: *An asymmetrical tone pervades a table pulled up to a window in a city apartment. Set to the side, the floral arrangement visually counterbalances the Oriental tea set. White dinnerware with colorful decoration is in sharp contrast with dark napkins placed—as becoming this table setting—off-center on the dinner plates.*

be supplemented with baskets to hold a selection of breads.

To complete this relaxed, family-oriented setting, choose flatware of sterling silver or stainless steel that is restrained in its design and decoration. Pieces of simple-lined, antique sterling will become instant heirlooms for your family. New high-quality stainless steel adds contemporary sparkle to your table. An excellent example is the beautiful "Shell" pattern from Gorham, which is clean-lined and unadorned except for a small shell motif at the top of the handle. Plastic-handled stainless steel will add a dash of color. Mikasa manufactures its "Continental" pattern in fourteen sophisti-

Sophisticated table settings can take a variety of forms. **Right:** *A contemporary room is a perfect backdrop for an eclectic setting that combines formal china, casual place mats and flatware with an Oriental-inspired centerpiece. Because they interfere with conversation, most designers eschew tall centerpieces. This one, with its simple lines and few elements, is an exciting exception that makes a striking visual impression and is certain to become the talk of the table.*

cated colors, including a lovely pale pink. A more vibrant flatware in this vein is from Gingko International, which is made in five colors.

You may want to serve wine with a family-style dinner but you may be deterred by the seemingly endless requirements for different types of glasses. In that case, pick an all-purpose wine glass. Several varieties are sold by most kitchen-specialty shops and department stores under the all-purpose label. Any of these will suffice unless you plan

a formal dinner. Another alternative is entirely different—the sort of glass used by wine tasters. These small, egg-shaped glasses are appropriate for several different types of wines: white, red, port, sherry, champagne, and even after-dinner liqueurs.

If you prefer to serve nonalcoholic beverages at dinner, select multipurpose lime-glass goblets that can hold iced tea or fruit juice for the adults, milk for the children, and water. A stunning stemware pattern available through Marimekko is

''Mariskooli.'' Pretty tumblers perfectly suitable for holding iced beverages are plentiful and, often, quite inexpensive.

Your choice of linens can either reinforce a casual setting for the family or inject it with a sense of elegance. This is helpful to remember as arrangements in many families are often made at the last minute to accommodate business associates as dinner guests. Though you may be caught off-guard when suddenly faced with unexpected guests, a change of linens can instantly dress a table up—or down—to evoke the appropriate mood. A pristine white cloth draped to the floor creates an elegant setting in itself. The feeling is heightened even more by adding an over-cloth in either a contrasting color, material, or type of fabric weave. For a dressier effect, add place mats in pretty pastel colors with beautifully detailed borders. A striking example is the mats manufactured by Le Jacquard Francais in cotton, linen, or a blend of these two textiles. Coordinating tablecloths are also available. A more casual feeling will be evoked by selecting rattan place mats. Though it may seem contradictory, this type of place mat looks wonderful when coupled with fine china, sterling silver, and lead crystal.

Regardless of the type of table linens you select, arrange the napkins in a traditional dinner fold. Begin by folding the napkin into quarters. Next, fold the napkin in half to form a rectangle. Place the napkin to the left of the dinner fork with the open edges pointing toward the plate.

A centerpiece of white tulips goes with any dinner setting. To add a splash of color, substitute pretty pastel flowers including pale orange ixia, pink alstroemeria, and vibrant blue-purple iris.

Center: *The traditional ambience of a Georgian-style table is enlivened with contemporary flair in the form of mirror place mats. The contemporary sensibility is underscored by wisely minimizing the number of elements in the visually rich setting.*
Below: *An antique lace cloth and a plethora of knickknacks and personal memorabilia recreate a Victorian atmosphere for a romantic dessert setting for two.*

A simple outdoor deck is quickly transformed into a setting for a romantic candle-lit dinner for two under the stars. A lushly colored tablecloth with matching chair cushions, crystal-clear dinnerware, and a simple arrangement of four candlesticks under the flowing canopy are the rich-looking essentials needed to coordinate this intimate setting.

Outdoor Dining

FOR PEOPLE LIVING IN THE COUNTRY, THE OUTDOORS is a natural extension of their environment. City dwellers, on the other hand, often have outdoor living space limited to a fenced-in backyard, a small terrace, or rooftop garden. Your outdoor space may be an expansive backyard, a spacious porch or a tiny balcony with only enough room for a few chairs and a small table. All of these places can become wonderful settings for entertaining family and friends at mealtime.

The first image that usually comes to mind is a casual setting perfect for a backyard cookout, especially when the table is enlivened with colorful glazed pottery. If this ware is your preference, you can transform the plates into liners by placing them on top of large terracotta drain pans that come with flower pots.

However, don't limit outdoor ware to informal designs. Just about any dinnerware you would use in the dining room is appropriate outdoors. For example, the beautiful plastics available today are perfectly at home outdoors. And more and more, people are taking their finest china outdoors and placing it right on a rough-hewn antique table. An excellent choice for outdoor dining is the sophisticated ''Blue Royale'' pattern by Lenox and ''Empress White'' by Wedgwood. Another idea for outdoor dinnerware is creamware. Imbued with the spirit of the old, creamware is an all-white ceramic that is frequently fashioned into interesting shapes. One of the collections offered by the Richard Norton Company of Chicago has eight-sided plates and matching serving dishes.

Even when dining outdoors it is crucial to

coordinate flatware with dinnerware. Plastic plates and serving pieces are often sold in sets that include cutlery. More sophisticated plastic collections—''Hellerware,'' for example—blend with informal stainless-steel flatware, especially if you select a simple contemporary pattern. As a rule fine china looks better when paired with sterling silver or silver plate. Beautiful sterling patterns for outdoor dining are ''Old English Tipt'' by Gorham and ''Pointed Antique'' by Reed & Barton. An excellent plated flatware is Oneida's ''Silver Shell'' pattern.

Sculptural glassware adds elegance to any outdoor table setting. A wide selection of inexpensive crystal is offered by Cristal d'Arques. A popular pattern manufactured by this company is ''Invitation Bouquet,'' which includes white wine and champagne glasses. Striking crystal tumblers are exactly right for serving highballs or iced beverages on a hot afternoon. Waterford manufactures nine-ounce old-fashioned glasses and tumblers in the ''Sheila'' pattern eminently suitable for these purposes. And keep ice for your glassware in a crystal ''Hampton'' bucket by Lenox.

Tablecloths are optional when dining outdoors. A pretty outdoor wood table can be left bare and place mats can be eliminated depending on your personal preference. Keep napkins simple in design yet plentiful in supply as outdoor settings often involve foods with sticky coatings such as barbecue sauce. In fact, absorbent kitchen towels of one hundred percent cotton may be the safest bet.

Arrange fresh flowers from the garden in a low-scaled centerpiece in either a ceramic or clear glass vase. Early in the growing season, place buds in small vases and set at individual place settings.

CHANGING SETTINGS FOR CHANGING SEASONS

W hat's your favorite time of year? Is it spring when the fragrance of blossoming flowers fills the air, or do you prefer the brilliant colors of fall as the leaves change? Perhaps you are a summer person who loves picnics at the beach or a winter sports buff who thrives on crisp, dry air and the challenge of a steep ski slope.

Regardless of your preference, emphasize the various times of the year by carefully planning menus to highlight seasonal specialties. Then complement your meals—and echo the season—by devising special table settings. This way, the look of your dining table will continually evolve.

You can imbue your table with the spirit of spring by selecting dinnerware and linens awash with the soft colors of nature: pastel greens, pinks, and blues. At other times you may want to contrast your table setting with the season. For example, an excellent strategy to eliminate wintertime blues caused by depressing grey skies and bare vegetation is to set the table with plates and napkins in vivid primary colors. Indeed, there are countless ways to visually blend your table setting with the season.

Winter

FOR MANY PEOPLE WINTER IS THE SEASON OF THEIR discontent. The skies seem to be permanently grey; the streets and pavements are coated with a veneer of slush and snow. However, many others revel in the weather of winter. They enjoy outdoor sports— skiing, hockey, and ice skating—or simply take long walks with the dog trailing behind.

Depending on your mood, you can evoke the spirit of fire or ice on your table. If you spend all winter huddled indoors daydreaming about a long holiday on a sunny beach, make the fantasy come to life. You can do exactly that, at least at mealtime, by imbuing the table—or a nook by the fireplace hearth—with a sense of tropical zest. For stylist L.A. Clever of Houston that means setting the tone with a cloth of red and burnt orange accompanied by bright red napkins with vibrantly colored Fiestaware from the 1940s. Plentiful and inexpensive in the days immediately following World War II, this simple, sculptural ceramic has gained a whole new following in the 1980s. To find Fiestaware, haunt flea markets and shops specializing in nostalgia or 1950s merchandise. Be aware, however, that the renewed popularity of Fiestaware has caused prices to soar. As an alternative to the real thing, you can buy contemporary ceramic dinnerware manufactured in the style of Fiestaware from kitchen-specialty stores. These contemporary wares have two big advantages: a greater selection of colors and lower cost.

Reinforce the sculptural quality of Fiestaware and other simple ceramics with stark contemporary-lined stainless-steel flatware. The designs of Scandinavia meet this need admirably. For example, you can mix one of the beautiful flatware patterns by Georg Jensen with the Fiestaware. Complete this casual table setting by shopping for colorful ceramic goblets in solid colors.

You may prefer a more sophisticated setting employing the same motifs. In that case, substitute a classic china pattern such as the beautiful blue ''Real Old Willow'' collection by Royal Doulton for the Fiestaware. Round out this setting with lead-crystal goblets by Kosta Boda in the ''Rainbow'' pattern. This lively design is decorated with swirls of primary colors.

With either of these place settings you can use bowls and platters made of woven rattan. A mass of thirty to forty votive candles will supply sufficient lighting. Set aside enough candles so that you can place one in the center of each plate, thus giving your guests a small memento of the occasion to take home.

An icelike table setting celebrates the winter season with magical glitter. Set the tone with etched, rippled glass serving plaques. If you wish, these plaques can be used as dinner plates. Several other lovely pieces in this vein suitable for serving only are sold by Tiffany & Company. Economical frosted glass dinnerware products are sold by kitchen-supply stores in many cities. Or select clear crystal plates manufactured by Arcoroc. Besides being inexpensive, they can double as liner plates for other types of ceramic dinnerware.

Continue your ice-like winter table theme with crystal stemware. Wine glasses with balloon-shaped bowls are visually striking and versatile. Besides holding wine, they

Basking in the warmth of the fireplace, this winter setting is quietly stunning with its classic symmetrical design consisting of formal china, lead-crystal glassware and beautiful flatware. The woven place mat strikes an unexpected yet delightful note of informality.

are suitable for serving chic desserts such as mousse. As an alternative frosted glasses are reminiscent of the wintry scene your guests have left outside and will add a sparkle to the table.

Selecting simple, even austere, flatware will impart elegance to your setting while furthering the overall theme. Christofle manufactures a wonderful silver-plated pattern exactly in this style called ''Malmaison.'' Classic in shape, the forks and

spoons in this pattern are outlined with a thin band of detailing. The circular-handled knife is unadorned except for subtle touches of decoration at each end.

Napkins of crisp white linen or cotton will complete your tabletop ice palace. A centerpiece of birds of paradise will surprise your guests and save this setting from becoming too severe by adding exactly the right note of color without detracting from the overall theme.

Above: *A pair of bunnies keep watchful eyes on a welcoming afternoon tea setting for three. So they won't interfere with conversation, the unusually tall candleholders are set to the side, leaving space for a lovely—and edible—centerpiece. The crocheted decoration of the tablecloth is echoed in the napkins.* **Below:** *A spring dinner becomes a memorable event when the table is a colorful mix of lavender and green.*

The color scheme is carried through in the dinnerware, linens, candles, and centerpiece.

Spring

SPRING IS THE MOST WELCOME SEASON OF ALL. After a long, hard winter, we exult in the renewal of life. The air is filled with the fragrance of blooming flowers whose bright colors excite the eye. Well-tended gardens overflowing with fresh vegetables encourage us to share the bounty of the season with friends.

As a result, many of us consider spring the perfect season to host a dinner party or a weekend luncheon. Begin by planning a menu that highlights fresh—and nutritious—vegetables and fruits. Then blend them into a table setting that reinforces the festive nature of the season.

An idea equally applicable indoors or out is a spring garden theme. Visually anchor your table with plates in a delicate floral design. There are probably more china patterns with this sort of motif than any other and one of the lovliest is the ''Fleur d'Eau'' pattern of Ceralene, a line of fine French porcelain manufactured in France by A. Raynaud & Cie. If you prefer, reserve the floral plates for dessert and place them on undecorated dinner plates. This way the color and design of the dessert plates are literally framed and, thus, emphasized by the rim of the plain dinner service below.

Flank your dinnerware with simple sterling-silver or silver-plated flatware. Because it draws attention to the dinnerware, a flatware pattern with restrained decoration works best in this setting. For this purpose, ''Grand Colonial'' by Wallace-International in sterling and Oneida's ''Silver Shell'' silver plate are the perfect classic shapes.

Linens should also be visually subtle. In-

stead of colored linens, choose classic white enlivened with an intricately embroidered or crocheted border. Napkins and place mats or tablecloths look best in this particular setting if they match in terms of pattern, texture, or color. For a midday meal, arrange the napkins in a luncheon fold and eliminate the tablecloth. At night arrange them in a traditional dinner fold and add place mats and/or a tablecloth.

To complete the elegant look of your table, select sculptural crystal decanters from which you can pour wine into similarly styled goblets. Continue your use of crystal in the centerpiece with a clear vase filled with a variety of seasonal flowers from the local nursery or fresh from your own garden. Complete your setting with new or antique sterling or silver plate serving pieces to add a touch of glitter and elegance.

Spring is also the season of informal get-togethers. An informal family supper on Sunday evening is a relaxing way to wind down the weekend and mentally prepare for the workweek ahead. An easy main course, a hearty stew, for example, can be prepared ahead of time and reheated for dinner. Or you can prepare a lighter main course right at the table in a chafing dish. Supplement either of these entrees with a selection of tasty cheeses and breads.

Mirror this casual meal with an equally informal yet visually pleasing table setting. Begin by draping the table with a solid-colored cloth that hangs to the floor. Next, form the base of each place setting with stainless-steel service plates that immediately set an informal tone for the meal. Soften the visual impact of the metal service plate by crowning it with a dinner plate in a solid color terracotta. The color of the dinner plate should, for maximum effect,

match or coordinate with the tablecloth. If you opt to serve stew, place stainless-steel porringers that match the service plate inside the dinner plate. Both stainless-steel service plates and porringers are widely available at retail.

The need for serving dishes is minimal. Stew is less likely to be spilled if it is ladled into bowls in the kitchen and carried on a tray into the dining area. A chafing dish can be lifted off its base and double as a serving piece for the host or hostess. You will, however, need a tray to hold cheese. Fortunately, the selection available to you seems nearly limitless and includes many beautiful woven trays and baskets originally intended for other purposes.

Breads also can be placed in a woven basket lined with a napkin to keep them warm. If you are serving breads at room temperature, dispense with a basket and arrange them in an antique tin or lacquered box. This small touch adds a note of sophistication to your table without overwhelming the casual feeling you want to establish. Old tins and boxes are abundant at antiques and secondhand shops in a range of prices dictated by the quality of the lacquer work or the rarity of the design.

Simple, clear glassware, French-inspired, one-liter wine decanters, and plastic-handled flatware coordinate nicely with an informal setting. Though many varieties of this flatware are manufactured, an exceptionally lovely example is the "New Winchester" pattern by Oxford Hall. This pattern is a deft combination of ivory-colored plastic handles and quality stainless steel. Complete this informal table setting with the sophisticated touch of large vanilla-colored candles placed in large round hurricane lamps that match handles of the flatware.

Above: A pale palette of blue and white is the perfect foil for a setting that leaves center stage to watermelon, that perennial summer favorite. Here formal dinnerware and casual fare are blended with flair. Below: Small touches give a light summer lunch of fruit a great sense of style. Though the meal is simple, it is presented with both serving and luncheon plates, lovely napkins held by green vines, and footed goblets containing dessert.

Summer

THERE'S NO DOUBT ABOUT IT—SUMMERTIME IS OUT-door time. This is the season we indulge ourselves with picnics and beach parties, good times around the swimming pool, backyard cookouts or simply lazy weekend afternoons spent in a hammock. For almost all of us summer calls for easy menus prepared far in advance. Cold meals of chicken, ham, and lots of salads and fruits keep the kitchen cool.

Many of us are also tempted to move our meals outdoors. Whether you follow this custom or simply bring the outdoors inside via flowers and floral table linens, this is the season to set your table with riotous colors. To start, cover the table—indoors or out—with a sprightly floral-patterned cloth of pinks, reds, and greens. Add napkins made of the same fabric.

Against this colorful background, simple

white ceramic serving bowls and platters will look striking. Two stunning patterns are ''Rosette'' and ''Fleur de Paris'' by Fitz and Floyd, the renowned dinnerware company. The ''Rosette'' pattern is a solid ceramic decorated with motifs resembling lattice-work around the outer sides. The top edge is scalloped, which adds to this pattern's sense of intricate detailing.

Complement the white ceramic serving dishes with white dinner plates decorated with ribbing around the outer edges. This type of ware is also fine for informal lunch-eons and family breakfasts all year long. A distinctive china pattern with a different and innovative look is the ''Tavola'' pattern by Hutschenreuther. Each piece has rounded edges that fan out to become handles on either side, which makes it easy to carry from the kitchen to the terrace.

Flatware of clean-lined design adds to the informality of any summer table setting. The natural choice for material is easy-care stainless steel, which, unlike sterling silver, requires no polishing. Contemporary patterns work best as they—and the dinnerware—draw attention to the tablecloth. More elaborate patterns should be avoided as they are too ornate for this inherently informal approach to dining. Two very striking contemporary stainless-steel flatware patterns on the market are ''Palisander'' by Lauffer and ''Grand Ribbon'' by WMF of America. The ''Palisander'' pattern has wooden handles that contrast nicely with the stainless steel. ''Grand Ribbon'' has detailing that simulates the look of a ribbon completely surrounding the handles along the edge.

Clear crystal wine glasses or goblets add sparkle while a centerpiece composed of large pots of begonias reinforces the floral theme. If you are dining after dark, add tall, colored tapers in crystal candlesticks by Orrefors.

Though we think of summer as an inherently casual season, it is an excellent time of year to entertain more formally. An elegant luncheon or afternoon tea in a shady grape arbor or under an expansive old oak tree punctuates the season with a sense of elegance. In the same manner, a dressy dinner party during summer's last weekend fittingly brings the season to a close and heralds the beginning of autumn.

For the event, cover the table with a bright cloth in one of the striking colors of summer such as sky blue in a subtle, latticework or checked pattern. China that is color coordinated—a blue floral pattern on a white ground, for example—will complete the summer ambience you want. Particularly suitable for the summer season in both design and name is the ''Forget-Me-Not'' pattern by Aynsley. If you prefer a solid design, an alternative is ''Blue Skies'' by Block China. This pretty pattern has a white center surrounded by a wide blue band on the rim. An entirely different sort of blue banding decorates the ''Marbre Bleu'' china pattern by Haviland Limoges. As its name implies, this design is imbued with a marbling effect in the blue border. The rim is decorated with a thin band of gold.

Here is an opportunity to enjoy vermeil flatware. Supreme Cutlery manufactures the ''Manchester'' pattern that is plated with twenty-three-karat gold. Although the overall visual effect of this design is stark and sculptural, the pieces are decorated with subtle detailing around the edges of the handles that soften their impact and imbue the flatware with a classical air suitable for more formal dining. (This pattern is also available in sterling silver and in high-quality stainless steel.)

The visual lushness of this setting calls for lead-crystal glassware. You can adopt several approaches in choosing the best pattern for you. If you prefer intricately decorated stemware, you will probably enjoy collecting the ''Alana'' pattern by Waterford. This design has a clear base with decoration limited to the bowl, which has numerous detailed facets. However, a simpler design may be more to your liking. In that case, classically shaped glassware with little or no embellishment will more than meet your needs.

Arrange individual place settings around a clear glass vase filled with wild flowers in shades of blue and purple accented by one or two white roses.

Fall

The bounty of the fall harvest need not only be displayed through food alone. It is—at least symbolically—represented on the table in the majolica dinner plates stylized in a leaf pattern, the woven place mats that evoke a sense of the earth, and the "radish red" napkins.

JUST AFTER THE DOG DAYS OF AUGUST END, THE nights suddenly turn cooler. The early mornings are heavy with dew and mist, and the air has a welcome feeling of crispness. A drive in the country becomes an adventure of discovery at farm stands bursting with fresh produce. This is autumn, and what better way to celebrate than with your own festive, seasonal dinner?

Early in the season when the colors of summer are still predominant, incorporate them into your table setting. You can use a type of ceramic dinnerware called greenleaf dishes that actually simulate the look and colors of cabbages and heads of iceberg lettuce. These fanciful dishes are accompanied by pretty dinner plates enlivened by a ripple effect that will add a rustic air to almost any table.

The green-leaf-style serving pieces are outright fun. Some realistically simulate the look of cabbage with bright green leaves and white veining that ''peel'' back at the bottom to form the base. At the top, the ''leaves'' fan out to become an opening in which you can place dips or soup. Other low serving dishes designed in a similar motif hold appetizers, vegetables, and entrees. The key to a successful table setting that utilizes this type of ware is to select dishes that look as realistic as possible.

Offset these ceramics with serving spoons and forks of antique silver or silver plate. If that is not a viable option for you, new stainless steel in a Colonial pattern will suffice almost as well. Add a dash of pizzazz to this setting with multicolored striped napkins that can double as liners for rush baskets to hold bread.

Search secondhand and thrift shops for old, plastic-handled flatware from the 1950s. It is easy to tell these pieces from newer ones. Usually, the plastic of the older ware has cracked, creating veining that the manufacturers probably never expected. Some of these pieces also have bronze blades that will add distinction to your table.

Store drinks in a pewter wine cooler. You can find these, too, by diligently searching secondhand shops. Or buy one of the many new designs available that reflect the spirit of the antique.

Later in the season is the time to bring brilliant orange pumpkins, yellow peppers, and brown and red nuts to your table. Burnt orange place mats, napkins, and a table-cloth set an unmistakably autumnal tone. With this colorful base, combine neutral earthenware plates and bowls in clunky, country-inspired shapes. An appropriate choice along this line is old white ironstone. This type of ware has become very popular in recent years and, as a result, prices have risen accordingly. Before you go out and spend money, however, check the contents of your attic. Your grandmother may have saved an entire collection. If you are not that fortunate, many antiques shops stock ironstone. New tableware alive with the spirit of the old is manufactured by Country Gear in its Hartstone Gear Collection.

In choosing flatware you have two basic options. One is the formal look of antique sterling silver or silver plate. The most compatible is late-nineteenth-century ware that can be found at antiques shops. The other approach is rustic in nature—stainless-steel flatware with wooden handles. As a finishing flourish, search thrift shops for large, old stoneware or outrageously overscaled silver-plated serving pieces.

STYLIZED SETTINGS

Table settings are fun—and flexible. Add a napkin folded in the shape of a fan and your table takes on a festive Mexican air. Replace your everyday linens with those of antique lace and you create a Victorian atmosphere.

You can tailor a table setting in several ways. Many people delight in coordinating it with the menu. For example, a Chinese dinner inherently lends itself to an Oriental setting while a Christmas feast looks its storybook best served on traditionally inspired china. Other people mesh the table design with their overall decorating theme, whether it is imbued with the country spirit, the sheer fun of eclecticism, or the hard-edge, functional approach of the industrial style.

Creating a stylized setting requires careful attention to detail to avoid a disorganized—and disappointing—mishmash. Fortunately, today's styles fall into a few general categories. Within these style definitions there is a great deal of leeway in which to add your own personal stamp by planning your table setting around a favorite collection of china, silverware, glassware, or linens.

Center: *Gold-rimmed china, cut lead-crystal glassware, and sterling-silver flatware and accessories are coordinated in a simple yet enticing traditional table setting.*

Traditional

OF ALL DESIGN STYLES, PROBABLY THE MOST POWER-ful in its emotional pull is traditionalism. It is the spirit of tradition that makes viewing a Queen Anne or Chippendale chair a pleasure—no matter how many times we've seen them before. And tradition is the style that comes to mind when setting the table for the most important family occasions and, likewise, for our most revered guests.

If the spirit of traditionalism is your particular decorating preference, your selection of tableware is wide indeed. The grandest way to set a traditionally styled table—and one of the most expensive—is by using antique dinnerware. Begin with early nineteenth-century blue-and-white dinner plates by Spode accompanied by white Ridgway dessert plates and sterling-silver flatware, circa 1830. From the decade of the 1820s, choose a Newhall soup tureen as a serving dish as well as crystal wine and water goblets. Though rare, these wares are stocked, when available, by fine antiques shops. One of the preeminent sources for these pieces is Bardith in New York City. To this visually spectacular setting you can add an antique crystal wine decanter and papier-mâché coasters from the venerable James II Gallery.

Of course a more modern interpretation of the traditional style is also possible. Designer Gary Zarr, for example, sets a lovely table imbued with the traditional spirit by using simple crystal service plates on which he places a traditionally inspired china service such as Fitz and Floyd's "Old Imari" pattern. Many flatware companies render traditional patterns in sterling silver, silver plate, and stainless steel. Look through the

Left: *A crystal bowl holds a generous serving of caviar for one in this setting that is imbued with a neoclassical spirit.*

JEFF MACNAMARA, COURTESY OF VOGUE MAGAZINE.

selection offered by department stores for the one that strikes your fancy the most.

The same rules of thumb apply to crystal. Lovely inexpensive stemware is offered by a number of kitchen-specialty shops in a variety of shapes. And instead of searching through the antiques shops for authentic papier-mâché coasters, have a contemporary craftsman such as Joe Turner of Los Angeles make a custom set expressly for your table. Then supplement all of these pieces with simple terracotta pottery—ashtrays, cigarette holders, and flowerpots—to visually soften the impact of your traditional pieces and set a more casual, relaxed mood.

Above: *A crystal bowl flanked by candlesticks forms a classically balanced and colorful focal point for a table setting of classical serenity.* **Below:** *At a chic, late-evening supper for two, a traditional setting is brightened by the burnish of gold and an unconventional but effective placement of the centerpiece to the side.*

The glitter of lead crystal mirrors the opulence of a contemporary interpretation of the traditional style.

Center: *A sleek black table is the perfect foil for simple white dinnerware. The color combination is unabashedly contemporary, a feeling that is reinforced by the banquette seating.*

Contemporary

WHAT COULD BE MORE IN TUNE WITH THE TIMES than a contemporary table setting? Besides its obvious appropriateness for life in the 1980s, the elements of a contemporary setting are the most available—and diverse—in the marketplace. The result is that a contemporary setting is one of the easiest to devise. And with its inherent light and airy ambience, it is one of the prettiest.

Begin with the glitter of crystal glassware that can do triple duty as water goblets, wine glasses, and delicate dessert dishes. Baccarat manufactures several sculptural patterns that perfectly adapt to this look. Couple this ware with large service plates that are also made of clear glass. You have many choices from inexpensive items sold in housewares stores to the beautiful dinnerware offered by Tiffany & Company.

You might want to select a dinner plate of a contrasting material. The most common choice is ceramic. Beautiful "Singapore" plates with subtle coloring and patterning that reflect the contemporary approach to design are sold by Lorin Marsh in New York City. These plates are deep enough to double as soup bowls at lunch or as cereal bowls at breakfast. Depending on your menu you may want to add a soup bowl. If so, a choice perfectly compatible with contemporary plates and glassware is the sophisticated bowls made of terracotta designed by Elsa Peretti. Though perfectly round and symmetrical, the Elsa Peretti bowls are visually softened by a small indentation that resembles a crease. They, too, are carried by Tiffany & Company.

A contemporary table setting almost dictates flatware in a modern design. Simple,

unadorned shapes bring a sense of understated elegance to the table without overwhelming the setting with unnecessary decorative flourishes. For breakfast, lunch, and casual dinners, you will probably want to use a stainless-steel pattern. Dressier occasions call for the beauty of sterling silver such as the restrained lines incorporated into Salem-style flatware.

If your dining table is a modern design with a glass top, don't bother with a tablecloth. Instead, select plain place mats and napkins devoid of decorative embellishment. White linens create a stark effect overall; pastels hint of Postmodernism.

Left: *What's black and white and spiced with color? This modern dinnerware design is the answer to this contemporary riddle.*

Above: *A tall floral centerpiece and a display of fruit add splashes of color to this Victorian setting.* **Below:** *An antique lace tablecloth makes a fitting frame for white china banded with gold. The gold color scheme is carried through by the napkin holders.*

Victorian

THE VICTORIAN AGE HAS COME OUT OF THE CLOSET. Long despised and admittedly totally out of step with the Modernism that has prevailed in architecture and design in the twentieth century, Victorian decorative arts have recently enjoyed a hugely successful renaissance. To give your table the flavor of the nineteenth century, select genuine Victorian dinnerware. Striking examples of this tableware can be found at antiques and thrift shops. But, because Victorian artefacts are becoming more popular, their prices have also risen and a bargain is hard to find.

Today, it is much simpler to blend the older pieces and new tableware that reflects the spirit of the Victorian Age. Search through the shops that specialize in historic wares for an épergne, a tall centerpiece from which the Victorians arranged cascades of fresh fruits.

With this piece as the visual anchor of your table, be on the lookout for nineteenth-century sterling flatware. The pieces need not match; a complementary blend of different patterns adds distinction. New flatware infused with the feeling of the nineteenth century will serve just as well. Look for linen napkins, silver salt and pepper shakers, pink-and-gold dessert plates, and sterling-silver soup tureens. All of these are perfectly compatible with a Victorian theme.

Amethyst stemware and plates reinforce the nineteenth-century sensibility as do accessories including large compote bowls and decorative cachepots. Bardith sells lovely amethyst stemware while plates, compotes, and the like can be purchased from Nuri Farhadi.

At teatime, pretty earthenware with a cream-colored background and a blue floral decorative motif echoes the upholstery on a grand old Victorian sofa.

Center: *Imbued with natural colors, this Villeroy & Boch pattern is completely in keeping with the latest trends in tableware design. The marbling in particular is a motif that identifies these pieces as avant-garde.*

Avant-Garde

MANY PEOPLE RECOIL WHEN THEY HEAR THE TERM "avant-garde." Immediately, their imaginations conjure up thoughts of hard-edge, cold—even anti-human—design. The avant-garde is important because it is the cutting edge that keeps all living art forms—including the decorative arts—growing and evolving. Without it, stagnation sets in as designers simply repeat what was done before without considering whether things can be done differently, and better. Though this particular approach to design and decorating may be difficult to understand, once it *is* understood, it can be appreciated. Remember that once upon a time the Queen Anne chair was a radical development, too.

In tableware the avant-garde style of today faithfully mirrors the evolution of architecture and interior design. What predominates today falls into two general categories. The first trend is a continuation of the sleek functionalism of Modern design devoid of ornamentation. The second trend has been termed Postmodernism, which, when decoded, simply means Modern design embellished with historical motifs, often rendered in unexpected materials. When dressing the table, there's no reason not to mix the two.

Simple-lined stainless flatware designed by Achille Castiglioni for Alessi is no-nonsense cutlery that immediately sets an avant-garde tone on your table. Add serving pieces with a Postmodern flavor such as the "Bombe" creamer and sugar bowl in silver-plated stainless steel by Carlo Alessi Anghini, which were way ahead of their time when designed back in 1946. All of these can be supplemented by avant-garde

JEFF MACNAMARA, COURTESY OF VOGUE MAGAZINE.

Left: *Imaginative and provocative, these Italian plates combine the fine art of portraiture with the applied art of functional design. Decorated by a photo-silk-screening process, they are part of a series of 350 plates, all bearing variations of the same woman's face.*

objects of the 1980s such as a round tray by Paola Navone, a three-section dish by Carlo Mazzeri and Anselmo Vitale, an oval wire basket by Ufficio Tecnico Alessi, and the striking "Lobo" square basket by Silvio Coppola.

If you wish to establish an avant-garde mood, then keep dinnerware simple by selecting a casual china in all-white, and linens of pure white cotton. Also look for wares rendered in unusual shapes and materials. Keep an eye out, too, for decorative motifs that would normally appear in another medium or that are rendered in an unusual fashion, and stick to every day colors such as white or pastels.

A new development has enlivened the

With their fanciful motifs and vivid colors, these sophisticated china plates are sure to become the talk of the table, especially when paired with what might otherwise be mundane plastic flatware.

avant-garde scene in the last few years: tea sets designed by architects. Part of an exhibition that toured the United States in 1984, these tea sets evoke a wide range of imagery. Michael Graves' set resembles miniature buildings with unabashedly Postmodern overtones; Charles Jencks' set has pieces in the shape of Ionic columns; the design by Richard Meier recalls the work of Cubist painters while Alessandro Mendini's tea set resembles a cross between a Fabergé Easter egg and the spaceship that left E.T. behind.

Above: *The colorful tea service is reminiscent of the work by the Italian collaborative, Memphis.*
Below: *One of the hallmarks of avant-garde design is the presentation of everyday materials or objects in a new and inventive manner. For example, a clarinet strikes a high note as a centerpiece in this inspired setting by Fitz and Floyd.*

Right: *This pattern brings a rural landscape to the table.* **Center:** *Ragged-edged place mats and napkins reinforce the country feeling created by simple china decorated in shades of brown and blue.*

Country

IN TODAY'S MASS MARKET, THE COUNTRY STYLE rules the decorating roost. Whether it takes the English form with colorful chintz draperies and soft, upholstered furniture or the more primitive American frontier interpretation, the country look is found literally everywhere—from genuine rural surroundings to big-city, high-rise apartment buildings in the modern style.

If this is your style, you will have no problem finding a plethora of new and old table-setting products. The most obvious way to unmistakably establish a country feeling on your table is by setting it with spatter or sponged ware. Reminiscent of nineteenth-century prairie life, spatter ware has a white ground decorated with a color decoration that looks as if it was splattered on from a paint brush. Usually, the color is a primary red or blue, and sometimes brown. Old sets are most easily found at a second-hand shop while kitchen-specialty shops sell inexpensive new versions.

Left: *The country craze can also be found on paper products as this enticing pattern amply demonstrates.*

Of course, you have many other exciting table-setting alternatives infused with the country spirit. In an Old World vein is the lovely blue-and-white English Corningware. White ironstone is a traditional country-style tableware while whimsical green-glazed pottery in an extremely primitive—almost funky—herb design is a good way to evoke a traditional country feeling.

To accompany these distinctive types of dinnerware, select simple glasses and flatware. Clear glass tumblers visually work quite well, as do plain goblets. To bring the zestful flavor of the French countryside to your table, add a pretty wine carrier. For flatware, choose plain stainless-steel knives and forks or stainless patterns with plastic or wooden handles.

Art Deco

WE MAY BE IN THE MIDDLE OF THE 1980s BUT THE 1930s live again, at least in decorating. Because of its geometric shapes, straightforward chrome-and-steel materials, and classical references, the Art Deco style is riding the crest of renewed popularity. Fortunately, decorative elements from the 1930s are at home in contemporary houses that embody many design innovations of that period including open floor plans and glass window walls.

The feeling of the "Tuxedo" design by the famous architectural team of Gwathmey-Siegel for Swid-Powell is quintessentially Art Deco.

To establish an Art Deco mood on your table, freely indulge in the exciting materials and shapes from that era. In the thirties, decorative objects were mass-produced so a wide variety of dinnerware and flatware in excellent shape is readily available at many nostaglia-oriented shops. Be forewarned, however, that as the desirability of these objects has increased, so have their prices. Their fashionableness, in fact, has inflated the prices of many pieces far beyond their intrinsic value.

If you like the overall look but aren't particularly concerned with authenticity, select new wares that are either reproductions or adaptations of Art Deco designs. These, too, are plentiful on the market. You can set the 1930s tone that you want with Art Deco-inspired "Tuxedo" dinner plates designed by the principals in the architectural firm of Gwathmey-Siegel for Swid-Powell Design of New York City. Supplement these pieces by choosing fluted champagne glasses.

Sleek flatware imbued with the free spirit of the 1930s is the "Deco" pattern manufactured by Mikasa. Serve vegetables and other side dishes in silver bowls. An example of beautiful ware in this style is the Alessi Mayan silver "basket." A versatile ware, it can also double as a container for a fruit or floral centerpiece. At breakfast enliven the table with a sterling-silver coffee pot such as the "Deco" pattern by Christofle. The pot, which has a briarwood handle, is part of a set that includes a tray, cream pitcher, and sugar bowl. Austere "King Richard" candlesticks designed by architect Richard Meier for Swid-Powell Design will add an impressive finishing touch to your Art Deco table setting.

Center: *The octagon, a popular 1930s motif, is given a contemporary interpretation in this pattern by Fitz and Floyd.*

A blast from the past: Swirling white and rippled glasses and patterned dinnerware evocative of postwar America make an artful vignette.

Americana

EVERY NATION HAS ITS OWN DISTINCTIVE STYLE. What better represents the English point-of-view than the architecture of the Adam brothers, the furniture of Thomas Chippendale, or the table artefacts of the Victorian Age? Because of the historically close relationship between England and the United States, America has elements of all of these in its architecture and design as well as a wealth of indigenous regional styles. But when we think of Americana, what most readily comes to mind are the designs first developed by the New England colonists.

The American style is rich in decorative effects, and can be deftly incorporated into many homes whether they are in the city, the suburbs, or the country. Early American tableware and furnishings are closely related to the country style. Both styles are somewhat rustic in appearance and, thus, add an inviting sense of visual texture to the table. In devising a table imbued with the Early American spirit, begin by choosing pewter or copper service plates and place them beneath hand-painted ceramic dinnerware. Good sources for this kind of ware are individual potters and smaller companies. Plates decorated with a stylized rendition of a natural setting in the center, for example, ringed with intricate detailing on the rim in a shade of Colonial blue are particularly suitable.

Couple the dinnerware with plain wine glasses and water goblets in clear lime glass and one of the many stainless-steel flatware patterns on the market in which the knives have a curved, or pistol, grip. For a slightly more primitive country look, select wooden-handled flatware. A lovely new flatware pattern of this sort is the "Ragotta" pattern offered by the Ralph Lauren Home Furnishings Collection.

Serving pieces can vary. If you prefer a visually unified appearance on the table, complement the pewter service plates with serving pieces made of the same material. For visual variety choose spatter ware, ironstone, or even historically inappropriate—but visually perfect—majolica. Add a dash of color to this setting with place mats and linens in pale pastels.

Center: *Used as place mats, rattan trays seem to float in space atop a glass table in a simple—and chic—contemporary Oriental-inspired setting.*

Oriental

IT'S ALWAYS NICE TO WIND DOWN A HECTIC weekend—or one of those nightmarish days at the office—by leaving the cooking to someone else and ordering an inexpensive Chinese or sushi meal delivered directly to your door. And because you are saving lots of time that would ordinarily be spent cooking, you can take several extra minutes to design a delightful table setting in the Oriental manner that will complement the food en route.

Your work has been eased considerably as the market is literally awash with contemporary, Oriental-inspired dinnerware. You will find shelves bursting with inexpensive examples of this ware in many import shops. Department stores and specialty shops also stock Oriental dinnerware. Some of the loveliest are ceramic pieces manufactured in glossy black, reflecting this color's new popularity in fashion and decorating. For example, Fitz and Floyd of Dallas makes black octagonal china dinner plates and accessory dishes as part of its ''Total Color'' program. Celadon-colored china is also appropriate as are chopsticks, the traditional Oriental flatware.

If you are a purist you will doubtlessly prefer traditional blue-and-white china pieces. These, too, are available at many department stores and shops. New blue-and-white ware has been imported in large quantities since diplomatic relations with the Chinese People's Republic were established in the 1970s. Even though much of this ware is mass-produced, some of it is lovely. Because the quality of these pieces varies considerably, it is recommended that you institute your own system of quality

control when shopping. This is much easier than it would seem as the clearer the design, the better the piece. Avoid ceramics with designs that are blurred or appear smeared. Antique blue-and-white ware is surprisingly plentiful so finding the right pattern is easy—check the sources section on page 133 for shopping suggestions.

Supplement these pieces with brass service plates, antique china teapots, and table accessories. Hand-painted fans spread face up on the table add the final, authentic Oriental touch.

Left: *This setting is more sophisticated yet more traditional in feeling. Note that this dinner for two is also served on woven trays.*

Romantic

A GENEROUS USE OF LUSH, RICH FABRICS AND LAVISH decorative accessories are the hallmarks of what has become known as the "romantic" style of decorating. The imagery most often evoked is that of a nineteenth-century Gothic novel or that of more modern versions, like the writings of Barbara Cartland. When you interpret the romantic style for your dining table, establish the atmosphere with elaborate linens such as intricately crocheted tablecloths, place mats, and napkins. The more fanciful the detailing—scalloped edges coupled with double borders, for example—the better.

Dinnerware can be equally frilly or more sophisticated. Hutschenreuther of North Branford, Connecticut, produces a very pretty china pattern, "Baroness," that has a white ground embellished with pale flowers and matching double banding. A more austere dinnerware is also appropriate, especially when it is emphasized by being set atop contrasting chargers. A pattern that has banding around the rim but is all white creates a stylish, monochromatic effect. For impact, place the china on metal chargers.

The essential elements of romance—fire and ice—are symbolically represented on a dramatically designed table by an ice decanter and vase made in a mold decorated with bright red roses.

No setting is more romantic than a beachside dinner for two at dusk. The crystal wine glasses, lace-trimmed pillows, and napkins tied with a simple bow hint at elegance while the china and plastic-handled flatware are also suitable for everyday use. A simple meal of fruit and cheese is romanticized when it is laid with small candles in clear glass holders as a decorative effect and for light after sunset.

On a sideboard with an antique lace runner and an arrangement of wildflowers in a shell, candles add a flicker of romance to the room.

Hutschenreuther also manufactures compatible crystal stemware. A particularly appropriate pattern is called ''Gloria.'' The stems in this pattern are exceptionally tall, and are topped with bowls decorated with a narrow band of detailing near the lip that flares out forming a sculptural silhouette. As an alternative choose inexpensive clear crystal goblets and wine glasses by Cristal d'Arques.

Flatware can be elaborate or simple. Dramatically curved, pistol-grip handles are eminently suitable for a romantically inspired table setting. An entirely different atmosphere is created by contemporary flatware. A striking pattern of this sort is ''Guardian'' by Yamazaki Tableware of New York City. This simple ware is unadorned except for small rings of banding at the end of each handle.

Center: *While some people might lay their hearts at your feet, this table design throws subtlety to the wind and places them right on the dinner plates. This romantic Valentine's Day setting leaves no detail to chance—from the centerpiece where hearts abound to the china with its vibrant border.* **Above right:** *Besides signifying Valentine's Day, red and white also herald the Christmas season, particularly when accented with green. These colors make a stunning backdrop for the traditional blue china pattern.* **Center right:** *The inviting collection of picnic basics that have been attractively organized by stylist Kim Freeman are perfect for an afternoon at the beach.* **Below right:** *At a New Year's Eve dinner party, the most popular element of the table setting is undeniably the centerpiece—in fact, it's the toast of the town.*

SPECIAL SETTINGS FOR SPECIAL OCCASIONS

At times life can seem to be a series of celebrations. Throughout the year we mark the special occasions that give life zest. Everyone has a special favorite, be it Christmas, New Year, a birthday, a wedding, a relaxed picnic, or a casual gathering of friends around a cheerfully set buffet table.

If there is a single term to describe the atmosphere created during these special times, it is "festive," and this is the mood you want to evoke in your table settings. Many events call for traditional items that will limit what you can do with the setting; with others you'll be able to let your creativity reign. For some occasions, practical requirements will dictate the setting—a classic buffet, for instance, for a large New Year's gathering. Here are some ideas to create striking settings for some of the most popular occasions throughout the year.

Christmas

WHETHER YOUR HOLIDAY PARTIES ARE ELEGANT AF-fairs or simple family gatherings, the table you set at Christmas dinner should reflect your interests and your hobbies—antiques, collectibles, and other cherished objects. Begin by covering your table with an elaborately detailed linen or cotton tablecloth that falls twelve inches over the edge of the table or is draped to the floor. White is always in style as are the more traditional Christmas colors of green and red or a combination of the two. A wonderful touch is to find an old cloth with compatible napkins in an antiques shop. This approach reinforces the age-old spirit of Christmas for established families, while for newlyweds it creates an instant heirloom. As an alternative, shop for reproduction cloths in the spirit of the past.

Christmas dinner is the time to set the table with your best china, crystal, and sterling silver. The more traditional the feeling you create, the better. An excellent china pattern is Royal Copenhagen's "Flora Danica," which has a white background enlivened by a gold medallion in the center of the plates surrounded by intricately detailed banding on the rims. Another approach to setting the Christmas table is to select dinnerware decorated with seasonal themes and motifs. One of the most enduring designs is "Christmas Eve" china pattern by Viktor Schreckengost, designed in 1953 for The Salem China Company in Salem, Ohio. This pretty pattern is decorated with a colorful Christmas tree in lovely shades of green with angels, ornaments, and candles. At the foot of the tree is a wintery tableau of a New England town with steep-roofed houses encircled by a railroad.

Heirloom silver and a Christmas pattern on the china make for an extra-special holiday setting. The small gifts placed beside each plate suggest a romantic Christmas meal for two.

A crisp Christmas table is awash in red and white. The plaid bows are cleverly tied to the napkins to embellish the tablecloth.

Poinsettias in a woven basket form a beautiful visual anchor for this table setting with a country feeling.

Ornate sterling-silver flatware complements china beautifully. One of the best ways to find nineteenth-century sterling is to hunt through antiques shops and second-hand shops. New flatware designed in baroque patterns combined with intricately etched lead-crystal stemware will make for a stunning traditional Christmas setting.

What makes a Christmas dinner table setting truly memorable are the crafts and accessories that impart a festive air. A wonderful touch is to weave a magnolia-leaf wreath and use it as a base for a centerpiece of violet nosegays. Or you can lay garlands of evergreens directly on the table in an interesting pattern and ''dot'' them with tree ornaments to heighten the Christmas theme. On a casually set table or one that reflects the decorative spirit of Americana, a woven basket filled with poinsettia plants will add a sprightly touch of color, especially when paired with blue-and-white dinner plates and tartan-patterned place mats.

A tall, charming centerpiece is simple to make: On a large serving platter arrange white narcissus flowers and polished red apples. For a centerpiece with a lower profile put a boxwood wreath on the table as a nest for a collection of gold-colored Christmas ornaments embellished with ribbons. To personalize the table setting, write the names of each member of your family and your dinner guests on the ribbons in gold glitter. As a finishing flourish place gilt-wrapped party favors directly on or above each dinner plate.

Easter

THE EASTER HOLIDAY WEARS TWO FACES. BESIDES ITS religious significance for the Christian world, it also marks the beginning of spring. For this reason, it's easy to blend both of these aspects into your Easter table setting. For tableware use the finest quality china, silver, linens, and glassware that you have. In many families that means recycling the wares placed on the table at Christmas, which is fine except for those pieces decorated with yuletide seasonal themes.

At Easter, accessories are what make the table setting special. Begin by creating an extravagant centerpiece with as many spring flowers as you can find. The more colorful they are the better, as at this point in the year, almost everyone is tired of winter and ready for the fresh air and colors of spring.

If flowers are not readily available in your locale or are too expensive, establish the mood you want by visually anchoring the table with a woven Easter basket filled with gaily decorated eggs. The children in your family will love this approach, especially if you continue the theme with antique metal chicken wind-up toys and small stuffed toy bunnies placed on the table. A more adult variation of this theme is to use hand-carved wooden rabbits and ducks.

A formal table arrangement is shown with clear crystal, silver, and white-and-gold china. A casual air is added with woven baskets filled with dyed Easter eggs.

*The back of a boat
doubling as a buffet table
creates the perfect
ambience for a picnic
setting at lakeside. To
keep the mood casual,
informal ceramic
dinnerware coordinates
with lots of wicker
baskets to hold fruit and
cheese.*

Picnics

IS YOUR FAVORITE OUTDOOR RETREAT THE COOL shade of a forest, a sun-drenched beach, or your own backyard? Whatever your preference is, the requirements for a picnic are essentially the same—good food and great friends drawn together by a striking table embellished with the perfect gastronomic treats.

Establish the mood you want with a fitting picnic cloth. Spread over the ground, the cloth doubles both as a tablecloth and as seating, so make certain it is durable. The type that immediately comes to mind is that perennial favorite—a blanket. Of course you have other choices. A dramatic choice of cloth is an old rug. One woven in the style of the American Indian with geometric motifs sets a casual mood while an Oriental rug creates a sophisticated setting.

Picnic ware comes in a wide variety of materials and styles. An easy way to amass a coordinated collection is to buy a prepackaged picnic set. Look for one that includes pretty earthenware plates, stainless steel flatware for four, and vacuum bottles and canisters for food arranged in a wicker basket along with matching cups for drinks.

If you want to collect your own set of picnic ware, start with enamel dinner plates coordinated with plastic mugs. For an unabashedly upscale tone, select lacquered plates. Either of these settings will be greatly enhanced by adding cloth napkins.

For an unmistakably romantic picnic at the beach, stylist L.A. Clever of Houston suggests a setting visually anchored by a durrie rug woven in bright, primary colors. For beach use, however, it's not necessary to buy the most sophisticated weave—more

inexpensive ones are entirely appropriate as the rug will be thoroughly full of sand after a day on the beach.

Enliven this scene with equally colorful tableware. "Hellerware" in bright red is durable and pretty. Then add cloth napkins in bright blue or brilliant yellow and plastic-handled flatware in a mix of yellow and red. Give your setting a bit of sparkle with the glassware you choose. But instead of real glass, which becomes a serious hazard if broken at the beach, opt for the acrylic variety that comes in handy four-packs. Serve your dinner courses from large acrylic bowls.

Round out your picnic setting with a simple yet eye-catching centerpiece. Cut a ripe watermelon in half lengthwise. Let one half serve as the centerpiece in which you insert tall tapers that will provide a romantic glow. Reserve the other half of the watermelon as dessert.

At a backyard picnic, the floral centerpiece is placed to the side and supplemented by a "wall" of flowerpots brought from the garden. A more formal atmosphere is established by the china serving platters and dinnerware as well as the sterling-silver flatware.

Buffets

WHETHER YOUR PERSONAL ENTERTAINING STYLE IS casual or formal, someday you will want— or need—to host a buffet. This style of entertaining has become increasingly popular in recent years, and for good reason. It is much easier to coordinate a gathering at which guests help themselves to the dishes and portions that they want. A buffet also enables a couple whose table seats only four to entertain a dozen friends with ease. And, just as importantly, it eliminates the need to hire a maid or other household help to assist in serving a formal dinner.

At this type of party the buffet table automatically becomes the center of attention. Setting a buffet table requires careful thought so that the implements and dishes are arranged in a logical, orderly fashion. Also be certain to leave sufficient room for guests to circulate entirely around the table. This way, they won't have to reach across a heavily laden table and risk dragging a sleeve through one of the dishes.

Here's a good, common-sense approach to setting the table for your next buffet: Mark the starting point with napkins arranged in either a luncheon or dinner fold depending on the occasion. The next item in the progression should be a pile of plates, then the meat platter, and next to that, a serving dish containing the vegetables. After these items comes a salad bowl, a sectioned dish for condiments, followed by a breadbasket, then glassware and flatware. The beauty of this method is that guests can carry their napkin and plate in one hand leaving the other hand free to serve from the platters. In addition, guests are not burdened with juggling silverware or an empty

Compact and efficient, this buffet setting is arranged so the dinnerware, linen-wrapped flatware, and stemware are ready to be picked up as needed by guests.

A woven blanket is an unusual but enticing tablecloth for a colorful dessert buffet setting of fruits and coffee. The fluffed up bandanas are a casual, innovative addition that add to the appeal of this setting.

glass as they move around the table.

An alternative that makes a lot of sense is to fold napkins so that they become containers for flatware. This ''wrapping'' eliminates the necessity of holding several loose items. If you opt for this combination, place the napkin-flatware package at the end of the table as the last item to be picked up. To make this buffet serving package, fold the napkin in half so that it forms a rectangle. With the folded edge at the bottom, fold over the top edge of the upper layer to the bottom creating the pocket in which you will later place the flatware. Turn the napkin over and fold the left edge to the center. The last step is to fold this section over on itself until the napkin is arranged in a tidy package. Place the flatware in the pocket.

A subtle approach to a dessert setting is this one with the periwinkle-and-white cloth that offsets the copper color scheme on the table. The placement of the candles adds an asymmetric visual interest to the table.

In recent years manufacturers and craftspeople have begun producing special buffet dinner plates that greatly facilitate serving. Larger than traditional dinner plates, they enable guests to place the entire meal on a single dish, thus eliminating the need for separate plates for salad and bread that would make movement around the table and the room a logistical disaster.

For a dessert buffet, lovely square china plates and a matching china coffee service are a distinctive way to set an elegant tone for your party. These can be combined with ''Blue and Gray'' earthenware serving trays by Mark Lanzrein for Tiffany & Company, as well as Tiffany-produced sterling silverware.

Weddings

ONE OF THE MOST EMOTIONAL EVENTS IN OUR LIVES is getting married. A wedding is a public and family celebration of the beginning of a new life together for the bride and bridegroom. As most of us know, however, getting married involves more than just the wedding-day activities—it consists of a progression of events that culminate in the wedding ceremony and reception.

Everything, of course, is prelude to the wedding ceremony itself, and the reception that follows. The wedding reception can take several forms, but usually it is arranged as a buffet or a sit-down dinner. To set a striking buffet table, select a tablecloth of the same materials as the bride's wedding gown or veil. Embellish this motif with vases containing the kind of flowers that make up the bridal bouquet. In this setting the wedding cake becomes the centerpiece. Be certain to include a large punch bowl so that guests can toast the newlyweds. Set the table as you would for a standard buffet. (For details on arranging this setting, refer to the "Buffets" section of this chapter, page 122.)

More formal wedding receptions call for a sit-down meal, either a formal luncheon or dinner depending on the time of day. Tables for guests are set as though for elegant dining. (For details on this setting, refer to Chapter Two, page 50.) The wedding party sits at the bridal table. At the center of the table is the wedding cake. Place cards mark each setting except for those of the bride and groom, who sit at the head of the table. At the other end of the table are the bride's father and the groom's mother. Along the sides of the table sit the best man, ushers,

A wedding party need not require the finest china. This paperware design suggests a bride's bouquet and is perfect for an afternoon outdoor reception.

clergyman, groom's father, bride's mother, maid of honor, and the bridesmaids.

A reception held before the middle of the afternoon is known as a wedding breakfast. This particular celebration requires a hearty breakfast meal or brunch. (For details on arranging this setting, refer to Chapter Three, page 62.)

Birthdays

BIRTHDAYS ARE THE GREAT BENCHMARKS THAT TO A great extent define our lives—a sweet sixteen party, becoming an adult at twenty-one, and beginning retirement at sixty or sixty-five. While the importance of birthday celebrations lessens for many of us as we grow older and enjoy so many of them, every birthday is a monumental event for young children. At a children's party you can easily set the appropriate celebratory tone on the table by inflating balloons with helium and tying them with ribbons to each chair. Stick to strong primary colors or bright pastels as these will catch the children's attention.

In place of the balloons, or in addition to them, cover the table with a thick white paper tablecloth and set crayons at each place setting so that the children can draw. You need not go to the trouble of buying this sort of tablecloth—simply substitute heavy-duty white butcher paper. Your butcher or grocer will probably sell you a small amount of this type of paper inexpensively and, perhaps, give you a free sample. This type of paper, incidentally, is perfect for making a banner which will extend your congratulations to the birthday boy or girl and can be hung above the doorway. As a final fillip, sprinkle store-bought confetti on the table.

Tableware is best kept informal at a children's birthday party. Single-service paper plates, plastic mugs and flatware will do the job quite nicely and minimize the adults' clean-up chores after the festivities. Instead of sophisticated all-black ware, select paper products patterned with dots, checks, and plaids in the guest-of-honor's favorite colors. Your local party store, department store or even supermarket will stock them.

Though many of these ideas are appropriate for older children, they need some modification. Paper and plastic tableware is too infantile for children over the age of ten. So add color and sophistication to the table by substituting vibrant Fiestaware plates and durable stainless-steel flatware. Retain the paper tablecloth, if you wish, but eliminate the crayons at each place setting as this touch will definitely not be appreciated by children on the verge of adolescence.

For adult birthday parties, helium-filled balloons tied to each guest's chair create a vibrant atmosphere, especially when the balloons are all white, silver, or pink and anchored by matching silk ribbons. This is the occasion to pull out all the stops and enjoy using the best tableware that you have. For example, cover the table with a damask cloth on top of which you place beautiful china plates. A chic line of fine china is Ceralene that is manufactured in several lovely patterns by A. Raynaud & Cie in Limoges, France.

Couple your china with fine silver flatware and serving pieces. An unusual line of sterling flatware is from the French company, Puiforcat Corporation. Their visually striking flatware has a handle resembling intertwined vines embellished with shell-like detailing. Repeat your use of sparkling silver with matching candleholders or add a touch of glitter by selecting crystal. Beautiful lead-crystal holders are imported from Austria by Swarovski as part of its Silver Crystal Collection. Finish off this elegant scene with a silver-footed cake stand, server, and champagne cooler.

A birthday dinner party is a great time to send the centerpiece up, up, and away with bright, helium-filled balloons tethered to the table by colorful ribbons.

Napkin Folds

These folds are appropriate for cloth or paper napkins. Be sure your cloth napkins are starched and ironed. When using paper napkins, use a cool iron to remove any fold lines first, then firmly crease the folds you make.

BISHOP'S HAT	FAN	BUFFET POCKET	FLEUR-DE-LIS
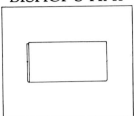	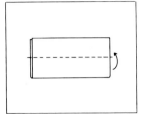	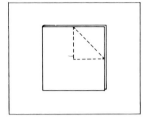	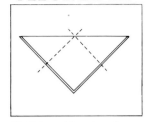
1) fold napkin in half to form a rectangle	**1)** fold napkin in half to form a rectangle; make another fold just like it and crease	**1)** fold napkin twice into a ¼-size square, open edges on top and right side	**1)** fold napkin top to bottom, and corner to opposite corner
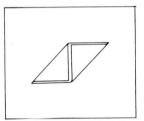	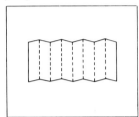	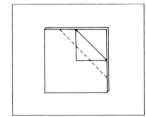	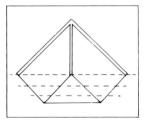
2) fold top left corner down to middle, and lower right corner up to middle	**2)** make 6–8 accordion pleats from left to right (you may need more folds for a large napkin); press pleats together firmly	**2)** fold down upper right corner in two thicknesses until the points are at the exact center of the square	**2)** fold two upper corners down to meet in the center, making a square; fold the two turned-down points back up to meet at the top
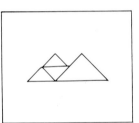	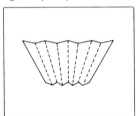	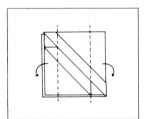	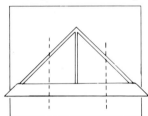
3) make a fold parallel to the long sides and pull up the two points so they are not inside the fold	**3)** with one hand holding the bottom, fan out the top with the other hand	**3)** fold down twice more so napkin is cut diagonally	**3)** fold bottom point up to meet the central edges; turn up or fold the lower part so that it overlaps the upper part by at least ¾", forming a band around it
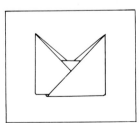	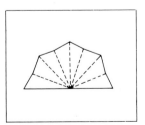	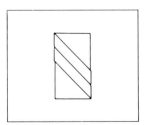	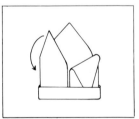
4) bend one side around and tuck in other side, then bend the other side around and tuck it in	**4)** place on dinner plate.	**4)** fold two more edges and tuck them into the pocket in the center, fold two sides under to meet in the back	**4)** bend from front to back and insert one point of the band into the other to secure them, turn down the two flaps and tuck them in

USEFUL ADDRESSES

(M): Manufacturer or distributor
(MO): Mail order
(R): Retail store

(T): To the trade only. Send inquiries to the address listed for retail outlets in your area that sell this company's products.

CANADA

Many of the products listed here are available throughout Canada at Eatons Stores.

◆ ACCESSORIES ◆

Bowls
CORANCO CORPORATION (T)
2409–46th Ave.
Lachine, Quebec
H8T 3C9

Brass and Copper
FRANS KOPPERS IMPORTS
LTD. (T)
1299 Kamato Rd.
Mississauga, Ontario
L4W 2M2

◆ DINNERWARE ◆

ASHLEYS CHINA LTD. (R)
50 Bloor St. West
Toronto, Ontario
M4W 3L8

GOEBEL CANADA (T)
100 Carnforth Rd.
Toronto, Ontario
M4A 2K7

HUTSCHENREUTHER
(CANADA) LIMITED (T)
55H East Beaver Creek Rd.
Toronto, Ontario
L4B 1E8

IMPORT & DOMESTIC
TRADING (T)
161 McPherson St.
Markham, Ontario
L3R 3L3
(Distributors for Mikasa and Dansk)

LEHAR TRADING COMPANY
CANADA LTD. (T)
600 Hodge
St. Laurent, Quebec
H4N 2A4

ROYAL DOULTON CANADA
INC. (T)
850 Progress Ave.
Scarborough, Ontario
N1H 3C4

◆ FLATWARE ◆

NATIONAL SILVER COMPANY
OF CANADA LTD. (T)
100 Toryork Drive
Weston, Ontario
M9L 1X6

NORITAKE CANADA
LIMITED (T)
90 Nugget Avenue
Agincourt, Ontario
M1S 3A7

◆ GLASSWARE ◆

ROSENTHAL (CANADA) (T)
55G East Beaver Creek Rd.
Richmond Hill, Ontario
L4B 1E5

◆ LINENS ◆

LAURA ASHLEY SHOPS LTD. (R)
18 Hazelton Lanes
Toronto, Ontario
(There are branches of Laura Ashley in Vancouver, Quebec City, Ottawa, Montreal.)

UNITED STATES

◆ ACCESSORIES ◆

Baskets/Bowls
AMERICAN HURRAH
ANTIQUES (R)
316 E. 70th St.
New York, N.Y. 10021

CONNECTICUT BASKET WORKS
(R, MO)
1262 Madison Ave.
New York, N.Y. 10128

COTTERILL & CO. (MO)
1119 S. La Brea Ave.
Los Angeles, Calif. 90019

THE COUNTRY LOFT (MO)
S. Shore Pk.
Hingham, Mass. 02043

FOLKLORICA IMPORTS, INC. (R)
89 Fifth Ave.
New York, N.Y. 10003

GORDON FOSTER ANTIQUES (R)
1322 Third Ave.
New York, N.Y. 10021

IMPORT SPECIALISTS, INC. (M)
82 Wall St.
New York, N.Y. 10005

MICHAEL R. JOHNSON, INC.
(R, MO)
410 Bellevue Way Southeast
Suite 2
Bellevue, Wash. 98004

SUE FISHER KING (R)
3075 Sacramento St.
San Francisco, Calif. 94115

ADELE LEWIS INC. (T)
101 W. 28th St.
New York, N.Y. 10001

KARL MANN ASSOC., INC. (T)
232 E. 59th St.
New York, N.Y. 10022

MATERIAL POSSESSIONS (R)
955 Lindon Ave.
Winnetka, Ill. 60093

F.O. MERZ (T)
225 Fifth Ave.
New York, N.Y. 10010

LEONARD DI NARDO (R)
Lambertville, N.J. 08530

NONESUCH GALLERY (R, MO)
1211 Montana Ave.
Santa Monica, Calif. 90403

SWEDISH COTTAGE COUNTRY
ANTIQUES (R)
1281 Madison Ave.
New York, N.Y. 10128

SWEET NELLIE (R, MO)
1262 Madison Ave.
New York, N.Y. 10128

THIRD AVENUE BAZAAR (R)
1362 Third Ave.
New York, N.Y. 10021

TWENTY SIX HORSES (R)
484 Broome St.
New York, N.Y. 10013

LILLIAN VERNON (MO)
510 S. Fulton St.
Mt. Vernon, N.Y. 10550

MARTHA WETHERBEE BASKETS
(R, MO)
Star Rte., Box 35
Sanborton, N.H. 03269

THE YELLOW MONKEY
ANTIQUES (R)
Yellow Monkey Vil.
Rte. 35
Cross River, N.Y. 10518

Candlesticks
COLONIAL CANDLE GIFT
SHOP (R)
Main St.
Hyannis, Mass. 02601

FAIENCE (M)
1555 W. Story Rd.
Houston, Tex. 77043

FLIGHTS OF FANCY (R)
450 E. 78th St.
New York, N.Y. 10021

FRESH FIELDS (T)
225 Fifth Ave.
New York, N.Y. 10010

METROPOLITAN MUSEUM OF
ART (MO)
Museum Special Service Office
Box 700
Middle Village, N.Y. 11379

Decanters
BACCARAT, INC. (R, M)
55 E. 57th St.
New York, N.Y. 10022

JAMES II GALLERY (R)
15 W. 57th St.
New York, N.Y. 10022

MARKETPLACE MANHATTAN
(R)
54 W. 74th St.
New York, N.Y. 10023

MARKETPLACE AT
SOUTHAMPTON (R)
42A Jobs Pl.
Southampton, N.Y. 11968

PIERRE DEUX (R)
870 Madison Ave.
New York, N.Y. 10021

Napkin Rings
ELEGANT ESSENCE (MO)
Box 15828
San Antonio, Tex. 78212

Place mats
THROUGH THE LOOKING
GLASS (R, MO)
41 Madison Ave.
New York, N.Y. 10010

Shakers
CARDEL LTD. (R)
615 Madison Ave.
New York, N.Y. 10022

CARTIER, INC.
Fifth Ave. at 52nd St.
New York, N.Y. 10022

Vases
ARTISAN GALLERIES (R)
2100 A-3 N. Haskell
Dallas, Tex. 75204

CONVERGENCE GALLERY (R)
484 Broome St.
New York, N.Y. 10013

FAIENCE (M)
1555 W. Story Rd.
Houston, Tex. 77043

NORA FENTON (M)
107 Trumbull St.
Elizabeth, N.J. 07206

FLIGHTS OF FANCY (R)
450 E. 78th St.
New York, N.Y. 10021

IITTALA U.S.A. LTD. (M)
41 Madison Ave.
New York, N.Y. 10010

LINDQUIST STUDIOS
GALLERY (R)
Patch Rd.
Henniker, N.H. 03242

SCOTT McDOWELL (R)
246 W. 18th St.
New York, N.Y. 10011

PHILLIP MUELLER (M)
37 Bridge St.
Brooklyn, N.Y. 11201

MUSEUM OF MODERN ART (R)
11 W. 53rd St.
New York, N.Y. 10019

SOINTU (R)
20 E. 69th St.
New York, N.Y. 10021

TERRA FIRMA CERAMICS (M)
151 W. 25th St.
New York, N.Y. 10001

TIERRA ROYAL POTTERIES, INC.
(M)
7020 E. 13th St.
Kansas City, Mo. 64126

◆ CRAFT GALLERIES ◆

JACKIE CHALKLEY (R)
3301 New Mexico Ave.
Washington, D.C. 20016

COMPOSITION (R)
2801 Leavenworth
San Francisco, Calif. 94133

CONVERGENCE GALLERY (R)
484 Broome St.
New York, N.Y. 10013

CRAFT AND FOLK ART
MUSEUM (R)
5817 Wilshire Blvd.
Los Angeles, Calif. 90036

ELIZABETH FORTNER (R)
1114 State St.
Santa Barbara, Calif. 93101

GALLERY EIGHT
7464 Girard Ave.
La Jolla, Calif. 92037

TEN ARROW (R)
10 Arrow St.
Cambridge, Mass. 02138

◆ CRAFTSPEOPLE ◆

Baskets
KAREN HUBERT
6303 Dahlonega Rd.
Bethesda, Md. 20816

Dinnerware
NANCEE MEEKER
Box 169
Rhinecliff, N.Y. 12574

TOM TURNER
415 N. Medina Line Rd.
Medina, Ohio 44256

Metal Flatware
RICHARD MAFONG
Art Dept.
Georgia State Univ.
University Plaza
Atlanta, Ga. 30303

SUSAN NOLAND
902 42nd St.
Des Moines, Iowa 50312

Papier-Mâché Accessories
JOE TURNER
8600 Burton Way
Los Angeles, Calif. 90048

Place mats
BOBBI BENNIS
7 E. 80th St.
New York, N.Y. 10021

Teapots
RAGNAR DIXON NAESS
201 E. 62nd St.
New York, N.Y. 10021

**Wooden Dinnerware (Bowls,
Plates, etc.)**
BOB STOCKSDALE
2145 Oregon St.
Berkeley, Calif. 94705

◆ DINNERWARE ◆

(Many companies that manufacture
dinnerware also make serving pieces
in the same patterns as well as
separate collections of flatware and
glassware.)

ARZBERG (M)
100 Shaw Rd.
North Branford, Conn. 06471

ANCHOR-HOCKING (M)
Lancaster, Ohio 43130

AYNSLEY CHINA (M)
225 Fifth Ave.
New York, N.Y. 10010

LEE BAILEY (R)
(at Henri Bendel, Inc.)
10 W. 57th St.
New York, N.Y. 10019

BARDITH LTD. (R)
901 Madison Ave.
New York, N.Y. 10021

BARNEY'S NEW YORK (R)
Seventh Avenue at 17th St.
New York, N.Y. 10011

DAVID BARRETT LTD. (T)
979 Third Ave.
New York, N.Y. 10022

BEDFORD-GREEN ANTIQUES (R)
Village Green
Bedford, N.Y. 10506

HENRI BENDEL, INC. (R)
10 W. 57th St.
New York, N.Y. 10019

BENNINGTON POTTERS (R, M)
324 County St.
Bennington, Vt. 05201

BERNARDAUD PORCELAINS DE
LIMOGES (M)
41 Madison Ave.
New York, N.Y. 10010

BLOCK CHINA CORP. (M)
11 E. 26th St.
New York, N.Y. 10010

THE BRASS TREE (R)
9044 Burton Way
Beverly Hills, Calif. 90211

NANCY BROUS LTD. (T)
979 Third Ave.
New York, N.Y. 10022

BULLOCK'S (R)
Seventh & Hill Sts.
Los Angeles, Calif. 90005

CACHE-CACHE LTD. (R)
758 Madison Ave.
New York, N.Y. 10021

CONRAN'S, INC. (R)
160 E. 54th St.
New York, N.Y. 10022

CORNING DESIGNS (M)
Grayrock Rd. & Center St.
Clinton, N.J. 08809

CRATE & BARREL (R)
850 N. Michigan Ave.
Chicago, Ill. 60611

CREATIVE RESOURCES, INC. (R)
24 W. 57th St., #603
New York, N.Y. 10019

DANSK INTERNATIONAL
DESIGN (M)
Radio Circle
Mt. Kisco, N.Y. 10549

DEMA HOUSEWARES DIVISION
(T)
DEMA TABLEWARE INC.
130 Campus Plaza
Edison, N.J. 08818

ELAN (R, MO)
Trump Tower
725 Fifth Ave.
New York, N.Y. 10022

THE ENGLISH WAY (R)
115 E. 60th St.
New York, N.Y. 10022

FITZ AND FLOYD (M)
1371 Round Table Dr.
Dallas, Tex. 75247

FORREST JONES, INC. (R)
3274 Sacramento St.
San Francisco, Calif. 94115

FOSTER-INGERSOLL (R)
805 N. La Cienega Blvd.
Los Angeles, Calif. 90069

THE FOUR SEASONS (R)
35 S. Middleneck Rd.
Great Neck, N.Y. 11021

GEARY'S (R)
351 N. Beverly Dr.
Beverly Hills, Calif. 90210

RICHARD-GINORI (M)
711 Fifth Ave.
New York, N.Y. 10022

GOEBEL U.S. (M)
Rte. 31, Box 10
Pennington, N.J. 08534

GUMP'S (R)
250 Post
San Francisco, Calif. 94108

9560 Wilshire Blvd.
Los Angeles, Calif. 90212

N.S. GUSTIN CO. (T)
225 Fifth Ave.
New York, N.Y. 10010

THE HALL CHINA CO. (M)
East Liverpool, Ohio 43920

HUTSCHENREUTHER CORP.
(T, M)
41 Madison Ave.
New York, N.Y. 10010

ILONA GALLERY (R)
31065 Orchard Lake Rd.
Farmington Hills, Mich. 48108

INTERNATIONAL CHINA (M)
41 Madison Ave.
New York, N.Y. 10010

JACQUES JUGEAT, INC. (T)
225 Fifth Ave.
New York, N.Y. 10010
(Robert Haviland & C. Parlon,
Howard Kaplan, Louis Lourioux,
Longchamp)

JOHNSON BROTHERS (T)
41 Madison Ave.
New York, N.Y. 10010

HOWARD KAPLAN'S FRENCH
COUNTRY ANTIQUES (R)
35 E. 10th St.
New York, N.Y. 10003

KELTER-MALCE ANTIQUES (R)
361 Bleecker St.
New York, N.Y. 10014

SUE FISHER KING (R)
3075 Sacramento St.
San Francisco, Calif. 94115

KOSTA BODA USA LTD. (T)
225 Fifth Ave.
New York, N.Y. 10010

RALPH LAUREN HOME
FURNISHINGS COLLECTION,
INC. (M)
1185 Avenue of the Americas
New York, N.Y. 10036

LENOX INC. (M)
Lawrenceville, N.J. 08648

LIBERTY (R)
1513 Wisconsin Ave.
Washington, D.C. 20007

MARSTON LUCE (R)
1314 21st St. Northwest
Washington, D.C. 20037

SEYMOUR MANN IMPORTS (T)
225 Fifth Ave.
New York, N.Y. 10010

MARIMEKKO (R, M)
7 W. 56th St.
New York, N.Y. 10029

MARKETPLACE MANHATTAN
(R)
54 W. 74th St.
New York, N.Y. 10023

LORIN MARSH (T)
797 Third Ave.
New York, N.Y. 10022

FRANK McINTOSH SHOP (R)
(at Henri Bendel, Inc.)
10 W. 57th St.
New York, N.Y. 10019

J. GARVIN MECKING ANTIQUES
(R)
72 E. 11th St.
New York, N.Y. 10003

THE MEDITERRANEAN SHOP (R)
876 Madison Ave.
New York, N.Y. 10021

MIKASA (M)
41 Madison Ave.
New York, N.Y. 10010

MINTON (T, M)
1 Gilbert Dr.
Secaucus, N.J. 07094

MOTTAHEDEH & CO., INC. (M)
225 Fifth Ave.
New York, N.Y. 10010

RICHARD NORTON, INC. (T)
612 Merchandise Mart
Chicago, Ill. 60654

PHILLIP MUELLER (M)
37 Bridge St.
Brooklyn, N.Y. 11201

NEUWIRTH CO., INC. (T)
225 Fifth Ave.
New York, N.Y. 10010

NORITAKE CO., INC. (T)
41 Madison Ave.
New York, N.Y. 10010

DAVID ORGELL (R)
320 N. Rodeo Dr.
Beverly Hills, Calif. 90210

PANACHE (R)
714 Vernon Ave.
Glencoe, Ill. 60022

PAST AND PRESENT (R)
1000 Third Ave.
New York, N.Y. 10022

THE PFALTZGRAFF CO. (M)
140 E. Market St.
York, Pa. 17401

PICKARD (T)
41 Madison Ave.
New York, N.Y. 10010

PIER I IMPORTS (MO, M)
2520 W. Freeway
Fort Worth, Tex. 76102

THE POTTERY BARN (R)
10th Ave. & 23rd St.
New York, N.Y. 10010

RORSTRAND CHINA (M)
c/o Kosta Boda USA Ltd.
225 Fifth Ave.
New York, N.Y. 10010

ROSENTHAL CHINA AND
CRYSTAL (T)
621 Madison Ave.
New York, N.Y. 10010

JOHN ROSSELLI LTD. (T)
255 E. 72nd St.
New York, N.Y. 10021

ROYAL COPENHAGEN (M)
683 Madison Ave.
New York, N.Y. 10021

ROYAL DOULTON (M)
700 Cottontail Lane
Somerset, N.J. 08873

ROYAL WORCESTER SPODE (T)
225 Fifth Ave.
New York, N.Y. 10010

THE SALEM CHINA CO. (M)
1000 S. Broadway
Salem, Ohio 44460

SASAKI CRYSTAL (T)
41 Madison Ave.
New York, N.Y. 10010

SELANGOR PEWTER (M)
321 Central St.
Hudson, Mass. 01749

SIGMA MARKETING (M)
225 Fifth Ave.
New York, N.Y. 10010

SODAHL (M)
1955 Claumet St.
Clearwater, Fla. 33575

SPIEGEL HOME WORLD
CATALOGUE (MO)
Box 6340
Chicago, Ill. 60680

SWID-POWELL DESIGN (M)
55 E. 55th St.
New York, N.Y. 10022

TAITU U.S. (M)
2150 Irving Blvd.
Dallas, Tex. 75207

THAXTON & CO. (R)
780 Madison Ave.
New York, N.Y. 10021

TOGNANA (T)
41 Madison Ave.
New York, N.Y. 10010

TOSCANY IMPORTS, LTD. (M)
386 Park Ave. South
New York, N.Y. 10016

VILLEROY & BOCH U.S.A. (M)
Interstate 80 & New Maple Ave.
Pine Brook, N.J. 07058

VILLETTA CHINA CO. (M)
8000 Harwin Dr., #150
Houston, Tex. 77036

JOSIAH WEDGWOOD & SONS,
INC. (T)
41 Madison Ave.
New York, N.Y. 10010

WILLIAMS-SONOMA (R, MO)
576 Sutter St. (R)
Box 7456 (MO)
San Francisco, Calif. 94120

THE WILTON CO. (M)
(Wilton Armetale)
18th & Franklin Sts.
Columbia, Pa. 17512

WOLFMAN, GOLD & GOOD (R)
484 Broome St.
New York, N.Y. 10013

YAMAZAKI TABLEWARE INC. (T)
41 Madison Ave.
New York, N.Y. 10010

♦ FLATWARE ♦

HENRI BENDEL INC. (R)
10 W. 57th St.
New York, N.Y. 10019

CRISTOFLE (M, R)
680 Madison Ave.
New York, N.Y. 10021

EVANS-MONICAL (R)
2750 Kirby Dr.
Houston, Tex. 77098

W.M.F. FRASER'S (M)
225 Fifth Ave.
New York, N.Y. 10010

GEBELEIN SILVERSMITHS (R)
286 Newbury St.
Boston, Mass. 02115

GEORGIAN HOUSE
SILVERSMITHS (M)
c/o Oxford Hall Silversmiths
103 Westbury Ave.
Carle Place, N.Y. 11414

GINKGO INTERNATIONAL (M)
Box 435
Downers Grove, Ill. 60515

GORHAM (M)
333 Adelaide Ave.
Providence, R.I. 02907

GEORG JENSEN SILVERSMITHS
(T)
225 Fifth Ave.
New York, N.Y. 10010

KIRK/STIEFF (M)
800 Wyman Park Dr.
Baltimore, Md. 21211

LUNT SILVERSMITHS (M)
Greenfield, Mass. 01302

THE MARKUSE/SCHAWBEL
CORP. (M)
281 Albany St.
Cambridge, Mass. 02139

MIKASA (M)
41 Madison Ave.
New York, N.Y. 10010

THE NEWPORT GALLERY (MO)
Box 3097
Providence, R.I. 02907

ONEIDA SILVERSMITHS LTD. (M)
Oneida, N.Y. 13421

OXFORD HALL SILVERSMITHS
(M)
103 Westbury Ave.
Carle Place, N.Y. 11414

REED AND BARTON (M)
Taunton, Mass. 02780

RICCI ITALIAN SILVERSMITHS
INC. (M)
41 Madison Ave.
New York, N.Y. 10010

STANLEY ROBERTS (T)
41 Madison Ave.
New York, N.Y. 10010

JOHN ROSSELLI LTD. (T)
255 E. 72nd St.
New York, N.Y. 10021

SWEDISH COTTAGE COUNTRY
ANTIQUES (R)
1281 Madison Ave.
New York, N.Y. 10128

THAXTON & CO. (R)
780 Madison Ave.
New York, N.Y. 10021

TOWLE MANUFACTURING
CO. (M)
114 Addison St.
Boston, Mass. 02128

WALLACE-INTERNATIONAL
SILVERSMITHS, INC. (M)
15 Sterling Dr.
Wallingford, Conn. 06492

YAMAZAKI (M)
205 Chubb Ave.
Lyndhurst, N.J. 07071

◆ FLORAL CENTERPIECES ◆

AU NATURALE
2506 Main St.
Houston, Tex. 77019

M.M. FENNER CO. (R)
73 Warren St.
New York, N.Y. 10007

THE GREENERY (MO)
497 Carolina St.
San Francisco, Calif. 94107

NEW YORK BOTANICAL
GARDEN GIFT SHOP (R, MO)
Bronx, N.Y. 10458

SALOU LTD. (R)
452A Columbus Ave.
New York, N.Y. 10024

SURA KAYLA DESIGN
ASSOCIATES INC. (R)
115 W. 28th St.
New York, N.Y. 10001

TWIGS INC. (R)
399 Bleecker St.
New York, N.Y. 10014

◆ GLASSWARE ◆

ANCHOR-HOCKING (M)
Lancaster, Ohio 43130

ARABIA OF FINLAND (M)
5603 Howard St.
Niles, Ill. 60648

BACCARAT INC. (R, T)
55 E. 57th St.
New York, N.Y. 10022

BARDITH LTD. (R)
901 Madison Ave.
New York, N.Y. 10021

BARNEY'S NEW YORK
7th Ave. and 17th St.
New York, N.Y. 10010

CRISA CORP. (M)
1600 Justo Penn Rd.
Laredo, Tex. 78041

CRISTAL D'ARQUES (M)
(J.G. Durand)
225 Fifth Ave.
New York, N.Y. 10010

CRISTALLERIE ZWIESEL (M)
3 Odell Plaza
Yonkers, N.Y. 10703

CROWN CORNING (M)
Corning Glass Works
3014 Tanager Ave.
Los Angeles, Calif. 90040

FOSTORIA GLASS CO. (M)
1200 First St.
Moundsville, W. Va. 26041

HADELAND OF NORWAY (M)
c/o Bing & Grondahl
111 N. Lawn Ave.
Elmsford, N.Y. 10523

THE HORCHOW COLLECTION
(MO)
Box 819066
Dallas, Tex. 75262

HUTSCHENREUTHER CORP.
(T, M)
41 Madison Ave.
New York, N.Y. 10010

JAMES II GALLERIES LTD. (R)
15 E. 57th St.
New York, N.Y. 10019

JACQUES JUGEAT, INC. (T)
225 Fifth Ave.
New York, N.Y. 10010
(Lalique, Saint Louis)

KATJA DESIGN SERVICES,
INC. (T)
466 Washington St.
New York, N.Y. 10013

LENOX CRYSTAL (M)
Mount Pleasant, Pa. 15666

LIBBEY GLASS (M)
Toledo, Ohio 43666

MARIMEKKO (R)
7 W. 56th St.
New York, N.Y. 10029

MIKASA (M)
41 Madison Ave.
New York, N.Y. 10010

SIMON PIERCE (MO)
The Mill
Quechee, Vt. 05059

ORREFORS, INC. (M)
41 Madison Ave.
New York, N.Y. 10010

PILGRIM GLASS CORP. (T)
225 Fifth Ave.
New York, N.Y. 10010

SASAKI CRYSTAL (T)
225 Fifth Ave.
New York, N.Y. 10010

SOINTU (R, MO)
20 E. 69th St.
New York, N.Y. 10021

STEUBEN GLASS (R, M)
717 Fifth Ave.
New York, N.Y. 10022

TIFFANY & CO. (R)
727 Fifth Ave.
New York, N.Y. 10022

TOWLE MANUFACTURING CO.
(M)
144 Addison St.
Boston, Mass. 02128

WATERFORD CRYSTAL (M)
225 Fifth Ave.
New York, N.Y. 10010

WEST VIRGINIA GLASS
SPECIALTY CO. INC. (M)
Box 510
Weston, W. Va. 26452

WHEATON FINE GLASS (M)
Millville, N.J. 08332

◆ LINENS ◆

LAURA ASHLEY, INC. (R)
714 Madison Ave.
New York, N.Y. 10021

BELGAMER (R)
806 Lexington Ave.
New York, N.Y. 10021

BOBBI BENNIS (M)
7 E. 80th St.
New York, N.Y. 10021

CHERCHEZ (R)
864 Lexington Ave.
New York, N.Y. 10021

CHERISHABLES (R)
1608 20th St.
Washington, D.C. 20009

CREATIVE RESOURCES, INC. (R)
24 W. 57th St.
New York, N.Y. 10019

ELIZABETH EAKINS INC. (R)
1053 Lexington Ave.
New York, N.Y. 10021

EGGS & TRICITY INC. (T)
979 Third Ave.
New York, N.Y. 10022

FLOSSIE DESIGNS (M)
123 E. 37th St.
New York, N.Y. 10016

HANDBLOCK (R, MO)
487 Columbus Ave.
New York, N.Y. 10024

LE JACQUARD FRANCAIS
200 Lovers Lane
Culpepper, Va. 22701

MARIMEKKO (R)
7 W. 56th St.
New York, N.Y. 10019

MOSSERI INC. (M)
225 Fifth Ave.
New York, N.Y. 10010

PAPER WHITE LTD. (M)
Box 956
Fairfax, Calif. 94930

PIERRE DEUX FABRICS
870 Madison Ave.
New York, N.Y. 10021

D. PORTHAULT, INC. (R)
57 E. 57th St.
New York, N.Y. 10022

PRATESI LINENS, INC. (R)
829 Madison Ave.
New York, N.Y. 10021

PRIMITIVE ARTISANS (T)
225 Fifth Ave.
New York, N.Y. 10011

RALPH LAUREN HOME
FURNISHINGS COLLECTION (M)
1185 Avenue of the Americas
New York, N.Y. 10036

PARK B. SMITH INC. (T)
295 Fifth Ave.
New York, N.Y. 10016

TABLESCAPES, INC. (M)
853 Seventh Ave.
New York, N.Y. 10019

THE ULSTER WEAVING CO.
LTD. (M)
148 Madison Ave.
New York, N.Y. 10016

◆ PAPER AND PLASTIC WARE ◆

GEORGES BRIARD DESIGNS,
INC. (M)
225 Fifth Ave.
New York, N.Y. 10010

BROOKS BROTHERS (R)
346 Madison Ave.
New York, N.Y. 10017

FINE DESIGN, INC. (R)
11 W. 18th St.
New York, N.Y. 10011

HELLER DESIGNS, INC. (T)
41 Madison Ave.
New York, N.Y. 10010

PAPER, ETC. (R)
1966 W. Gray
Houston, Tex. 77019

PAPER HOUSE, INC. (R)
2216 Palmer Ave.
Pittsburgh, Pa. 15218

◆ SERVING PIECES ◆

THE AMERICAN COUNTRY
STORE, INC. (R, MO)
969 Lexington Ave.
New York, N.Y. 10021

BARDITH LTD. (R)
901 Madison Ave.
New York, N.Y. 10021

DAVID BARRETT INC. (T)
979 Third Ave.
New York, N.Y. 10022

DAVID BAUME LTD. (T)
979 Third Ave.
New York, N.Y. 10022

CACHE-CACHE LTD. (R)
888 Madison Ave.
New York, N.Y. 10021

COLONY GLASSWARE (T)
225 Fifth Ave., #1000
New York, N.Y. 10010

EIGEN ARTS (M)
579 Broadway
New York, N.Y. 10022

NURI FARHADI, INC. (R)
920 Third Ave.
New York, N.Y. 10021

MICHAEL FEINBERG, INC. (T)
225 Fifth Ave.
New York, N.Y. 10010

BETH FORER (M)
243 Riverside Dr.
New York, N.Y. 10025

FAROY SALES CO. (T)
225 Fifth Ave.
New York, N.Y. 10010

HALDON GROUP (M)
3245 W. Story Rd.
Irving, Tex. 70516

HAMMARY (M)
2464 Norwood St. Southwest
Lenoir, N.C. 28645

SUSAN LEADER (MO)
R.D. #1, Box 230
Chester, Vt. 05143

MITTELDORFER-STRAUS,
INC. (T)
41 Madison Ave.
New York, N.Y. 10010

SIR THOMAS LIPTON TRADING
CO. (MO)
150 S. Main St., Box 415
Woodridge, N.J. 07075

J. GARVIN MECKING
ANTIQUES (R)
72 E. 11th St.
New York, N.Y. 10003

ONEIDA LTD. (M)
Oneida, N.Y. 13421

P.S. EDITIONS (T)
225 Fifth Ave.
New York, N.Y. 10010

RUBEL & CO. (T)
225 Fifth Ave.
New York, N.Y. 10010

D.F. SANDERS & CO., INC. (R)
386 W. Broadway
New York, N.Y. 10012

MAYA SCHAPER CHEESE AND
ANTIQUES (R)
152 E. 70th St.
New York, N.Y. 10027

SIGMA MARKETING (T)
225 Fifth Ave.
New York, N.Y. 10010

WOLFMAN, GOLD & GOOD
CO. (R)
484 Broome St.
New York, N.Y. 10013

ZONA (R, MO)
484 Broome St.
New York, N.Y. 10013

INDEX

Page numbers in italics refer
to illustrations.

MANUFACTURERS' CREDITS

Below is a listing of some of the patterns shown in *Dining in Style*. To order, see the Sources list beginning on page 131.

Bing and Grondahl Inc.: p. 61 (t), ''Coppelia''; p. 82 (r), ''Empire''

Contempo: p. 47 (b), ''Fantasy''; p. 48, ''Viri''; p. 101 (r), ''Autumn Stensil''; p. 127, ''Forever Yours''

Fitz and Floyd: p. 19, ''Imperial Dynasty''; p. 20 (r), ''Crane with Pine''; p. 42 (c), ''By the Sea''; p. 59, ''Cloissonné Peony''; p. 90 (b), ''Dynasty''; p. 99 (b), ''After the Concert''; pp. 102–103, ''Art Deco''; pp. 112–113, ''Rondelet Rouge''; p. 118, ''Potpourri''; p. 126, ''Classique d'Or''

Gorham: p. 17, ''Chantilly''

Jacques Jugeat Inc.: p. 29 (r), ''Angel'' by Lalique; p. 36, ''Vase Bacchantes'' by Lalique; p. 37 (r), ''Bristol'' by Saint Louis

Reed and Barton: p. 15, ''Francis I''; pp. 38–39, ''Chippendale'' tray, ''Paul Revere'' bowl and pitcher

Swid Powell: p. 20 (l), ''Bellosillo Figure''; p. 37 (bl), ''Stars''; p. 102 (l), ''Tuxedo''

Towle: pp. 14–15 (left to right), ''French Gadroon'' (stainless and gold); ''Wood Lily'' (stainless and gold); ''King Gustav'' (stainless); ''Rue Royale'' (stainless); ''Beaded Antique'' (stainless); ''Silver Old Vienna'' (stainless); p. 25 (l), ''Estoril''; p. 44, ''Clifden''

Villeroy & Boch: p. 21 (l), ''Aurapola''; p. 77 (b), ''Indian Summer''; pp. 96–97, ''Siena''; p. 100, ''Vaif''

Wedgwood: pp. 18–19, ''Runnymede Dark Blue''; p. 23, ''Lancaster'' by Adams

PHOTO CREDITS

Bing and Grondahl Inc.: pp. 61 (t), 82 (r), 113 (t)

Bouchet, Guy (Kim Freeman, stylist): p. 61 (c)

Chestnut, Richard: p. 94 (b)

Chowanetz, Gary/EWA: pp. 84–85 (spread)

Contempo: pp. 47 (b), 48, 101 (r), 127

Crate and Barrel: p. 13 (t)

D'Addio, Jim: pp. 67 (b), 88–89 (spread)

Derrick and Love: p. 72 (l)

DosPassos, Sandra: p. 120

Dunne, Michael/EWA: pp. 56–57, (spread), 77 (b)

Eifert, Daniel: pp. 52–53 (spread) Katherine Stephens, designer; 72–73 (spread) Ruben De Saaverda, designer; 87 (b), 90 (t), 92–93 (spread) Rita Falkner, designer

Elliot, John (Samuel Botero, designer): pp. 116, 119

Elizabeth Whiting and Associates: pp. 76–77 (spread)

Ennis, Phillip H.: p. 105

Fitz and Floyd: pp. 19, 20 (r), 42 (c), 59, 90 (b), 99 (b), 102–103 (spread), 112–113 (spread), 118, 126

Giovanni, Raeanne (Kim Freeman, stylist): p. 47 (c)

Gorham: p. 17

Hing/Norton: p. 108

Jacques Jugeat Inc.: pp. 29 (r), 36, 37 (r)

Leatart, Brian: pp. 9, 26 (l), 43 (r), 109, 115, 129

Leighton, Tom/EWA: p. 33

Le Jacquard Français: p. 41

Levin, James R.: pp. 13 (b), 27, 28, 34–35 (spread), 45, 55 (t,b), 62 (t), 64, 73, 82 (l), 114 (b), 117, 125

Lewin, Elise (Kim Freeman, stylist): pp. 49, 110, 113 (c)

Lillian Vernon: p. 37 (tl)

Mackenzie-Childs Ltd.: pp. 25 (b), 39

Marimekko oy: p. 22 (t)

Motif: pp. 42 (l), 94 (t)

The Museum of Modern Art: pp. 13 (tc), 21 (r), 24 (b), 26 (r), 30 (photo: Dick Frank)

O'Rourke, Randy: pp. 29 (l), 40, 60–61 (spread), 61 (b), 62–63 (spread), 79, 111, 121, 122–123 (spread), 124

Nicholson, Michael/EWA: p. 47

Paige, Peter: pp. 13 (bc), 95, 113 (b)

Reed and Barton: pp. 15, 38–39 (spread)

Roseanne Raab Associates: p. 16

Ross, Richard M.: pp. 87 (c), 91

The Rosenthal Studio-Linie/The Haas Group: p. 99 (t)

Rothschild, Bill: pp. 32, 43 (l), 51, 52, 54, 67 (t), 70–71 (spread), 71, 74–75 (spread), 80 (t,b), 100–101 (spread), 106–107 (spread)

Rue de France: p. 69 (t)

Sachs, Jane: pp. 24 (t), 86–87 (spread)

Street-Porter, Tim/EWA: p. 98

Swid Powell: p. 20 (l), 37 (bl), 102 (l)

Towle: pp. 14–15 (spread), 25 (l), 44

Tubby, Jerry/EWA: 53

Villeroy & Boch: pp. 21 (l), 38 (l), 60 (b), 77 (b), 93, 96–97 (spread, photo: E. Akis), 100

Von Einsiedel, Andreas/EWA: pp. 46–47 (spread)

Wedgwood: pp. 18–19 (spread), 23

Williams-Sonoma: p. 25 (r)